Early Praise for
Modern Vim

I'm once again impressed by the limitless possibilities of this classic editor. It goes without saying that I would—and will—recommend *Modern Vim* to anyone using Vim, including admins, developers, and Linux enthusiasts.

➤ **Tibor Simic**
Software Developer, Ingemark

With *Practical Vim* I am able to move around my text like a kangaroo. *Modern Vim* puts a Swiss Army knife into my pouch.

➤ **Miroslav Šedivý**
Software Architect, UBIMET GmbH

Even as an experienced Vim user and plugin author, I learned a lot with this book.

➤ **Kassio Borges**
Senior Software Engineer, Zendesk, and author of the Neoterm plugin

If you're curious as to what's new in Vim 8 and Neovim, or looking to extend the collection of great recipes started in *Practical Vim*, this book is an excellent resource.

➤ **Eric Casteleijn**
Vim Enthusiast

Modern Vim

Craft Your Development Environment
with Vim 8 and Neovim

Drew Neil

The Pragmatic Bookshelf

Raleigh, North Carolina

Many of the designations used by manufacturers and sellers to distinguish their products are claimed as trademarks. Where those designations appear in this book, and The Pragmatic Programmers, LLC was aware of a trademark claim, the designations have been printed in initial capital letters or in all capitals. The Pragmatic Starter Kit, The Pragmatic Programmer, Pragmatic Programming, Pragmatic Bookshelf, PragProg and the linking *g* device are trademarks of The Pragmatic Programmers, LLC.

Every precaution was taken in the preparation of this book. However, the publisher assumes no responsibility for errors or omissions, or for damages that may result from the use of information (including program listings) contained herein.

Our Pragmatic books, screencasts, and audio books can help you and your team create better software and have more fun. Visit us at *https://pragprog.com*.

The team that produced this book includes:

Publisher: Andy Hunt
VP of Operations: Janet Furlow
Managing Editor: Brian MacDonald
Supervising Editor: Jacquelyn Carter
Development Editor: Katharine Dvorak
Copy Editor: Jasmine Kwityn
Indexing: Potomac Indexing, LLC
Layout: Gilson Graphics

For sales, volume licensing, and support, please contact *support@pragprog.com*.

For international rights, please contact *rights@pragprog.com*.

Contents

Acknowledgments

I'm grateful to have the opportunity to work with the Pragmatic Bookshelf. Thanks to Susannah Pfalzer for encouraging me to submit a proposal for another book on Vim. And thanks to Katharine Dvorak for all your help throughout the project.

This book could not have happened without the support of my wife, Hannah. I'm so grateful to you for believing in me.

Modern Vim also wouldn't have been possible without my technical reviewers. Each of you contributed something and helped shape the book. I'd like to thank Ali Alwasity, Kassio Borges, Eric Casteleijn, Tim Chase, Junegunn Choi, Javier Collado, Dave Copeland, Marco Hinz, Justin Keyes, Andy Lester, Janko Marohnić, Tim Pope, Steven! Ragnarok, fREW Schmidt, Miroslav Šedivý, Tibor Simic, Ken Takata, Tim Tyrrell, Andrew Wray, and Alex Young.

Thanks to the folks at thoughtbot, Ben Orenstein in particular, for commissioning a series of video tutorials about Vim and Neovim. This collaboration pushed me to begin working on the book and gave me a running start.

I'm always grateful to everyone who works on Vim, Neovim, and the assorted plugins that make my life easer.

The Neovim logo was designed by Jason Long, and is licensed under the Creative Commons Attribution 3.0 Unported License.[1] We've used the one-color flat variation of the logo, because it looks best both online and in print.

The Vim logo is copyrighted. Thanks to Bram Moolenaar for granting permission to reproduce a one-color flat variation of the Vim logo in this book.

November 2017 was an unusually fruitful month. On November 1, we published the first beta edition of this book. On November 2, my wife gave birth to our son, Conrad. I could hardly believe my luck.

---

1. https://creativecommons.org/licenses/by/3.0

Introduction

Vim's core functionality makes it a good programmer's text editor. Turning Vim into a full-blown development environment means combining it with other tools and extending its capabilities with plugins. In *Practical Vim [Nei15]*, I focused on the core features of the editor. In this book, I show you how to extend Vim and make it the centerpiece of a Unix-based IDE.

How This Book Is Structured

Modern Vim is a recipe book. It's not designed to be read from start to finish. Each chapter is a collection of tips that are related by a theme, and each tip demonstrates a particular feature in action. Some tips are self-contained. Others depend upon material elsewhere in the book. Those tips are cross-referenced so you can find everything easily.

Modern Vim doesn't progress from novice to advanced level, but each individual chapter does. A less-experienced Vim user might prefer to make a first pass through the book, reading just the early tips in each chapter. A more advanced user might choose to focus on the later tips or move around the book as needed. If it helps, you can think of this as a "Choose Your Own Adventure" book.

A Note on Vim Versions

To follow the tips in this book, you're going to need an up-to-date installation of Vim. (The clue is right there in the book's title!) You have two options: use version 8 of Vim or version 0.2 of Neovim.

Vim Version 8

Version 8 of Vim was released in September 2016. It introduced some new features that you'll learn about in this book, such as packages and job control. As a minimum requirement, you'll need to be running version 8 of Vim, compiled with the huge feature set. You'll find instructions on how to install Vim 8 in Tip 1, *Installing Vim 8*, on page 2.

All of the tips in this book have been tested with version 8.0 of Vim, apart from a handful of tips which have been written especially for Neovim.

Neovim

Neovim is a community-run fork of Vim that can be used as a drop-in replacement for Vim. It supports all of the same features Vim 8 offers and more. You'll find instructions on how to install Neovim in Tip 2, *Switching to Neovim*, on page 4.

All of the tips in this book have been tested with Version 0.2.2 of Neovim.

Terminology

In many ways, Vim 8 and Neovim are interchangeable. When I use the word "Vim" by itself, you can read that as "Vim 8," or you can read it as "Neovim." If I want to make a specific point about one particular version of Vim, then I will specify "Vim 8" or "Neovim" to make that clear.

If you see this signpost at the start of a tip, it means that the tip is relevant only for Neovim:

 Neovim only

If a tip only applies to Vim 8, you'll see a signpost like this:

 Vim 8 only

If you see no such signposts at the start of a tip, then that tip should work just as well in both versions. Most of the tips in this book work in both Vim 8 and Neovim.

Contextual Instructions Using $VIMCONFIG

Vim 8 and Neovim follow different conventions on where to keep their configuration files. Vim 8 typically places them in a ~/.vim directory, whereas Neovim uses the ~/.config/nvim directory. These are important details, but it would get distracting if I mentioned them every time I referenced a runtime file.

To avoid this problem, we'll refer to certain files and directories using environment variables $MYVIMRC, $VIMCONFIG, and $VIMDATA. When you see $VIMCONFIG, you can interpret that as ~/.vim if you are using Vim, or ~/.config/nvim if you are using Neovim. You'll find complete instructions on how to interpret these variables in *Contextual Instructions for Vim*, on page 3 and *Contextual Instructions for Neovim*, on page 7.

Other Software Requirements

In *Modern Vim*, many of the lessons are illustrated with practical examples. You'll learn best if you actually follow the examples, and in some cases that means you're going to need to run other programs besides Vim.

JavaScript, Node.js, and npm

Many examples in this book are illustrated using JavaScript, which has become something of a universal language in recent years. Even if JavaScript is not your first choice for a programming language, you probably know enough "pidgin JavaScript" to be able to follow the examples in this book. All of the Vim features that are demonstrated for JavaScript can be adapted for other languages.

If you want to execute the JavaScript examples in this book, you'll need to install the Node.js[1] runtime, as well as the package manager npm.[2] Check out their websites for installation instructions.

Bash Shell (Or Any Shell)

Some of the tips in this book involve running commands in a shell. The examples are written assuming that you use the bash shell, because this is the default shell on many systems.

I don't mean to suggest that you *should* be using bash. If you prefer to use zsh, fish, or another shell, that's cool. You've invested time customizing your shell, so you should be prepared to spend a little bit more time adapting my instructions to make them work for your setup. You shouldn't have any trouble with this, since we only use basic features of the shell.

Git

Throughout this book you'll find instructions for running git commands, such as clone, init, and commit. You'll need an up-to-date installation of Git. You can find instructions for installing Git online.[3]

---

1. https://nodejs.org
2. https://www.npmjs.com
3. https://git-scm.com/book/en/v2/Getting-Started-Installing-Git

Ripgrep

The Ripgrep tool by Andrew Gallant[4] makes a couple of appearances. Much like grep, the primary purpose of Ripgrep is to search files for a pattern, and you'll see it used this way in Tip 13, *Searching Files with Grep-Alikes*, on page 56. Ripgrep also has a neat bonus feature: running `ripgrep --files` lists all the files beneath the current working directory, minus those that are ignored by your version control system. You'll see this feature put to use in Tip 7, *Finding Files Using Fuzzy Path Matching*, on page 23.

Depending on which platform you're using, you may be able to install Ripgrep using your package manager. If that doesn't work, take a look at the release page on GitHub.[5] There, you'll find pre-built binaries for Linux and Mac.

Don't worry if you can't get Ripgrep to work on your machine. It's nice to have, but you can get by fine without it.

Notation for Simulating Vim on the Page

`Ctrl-s` is a common convention for representing chordal key commands. It means "While holding down the `Ctrl` key, press the `s` key." But this convention isn't well suited to describing Vim's modal command set. In *Modern Vim*, I use a specific notation to illustrate Vim usage, which I outline here.

Playing Melodies

In Normal mode, commands are composed by typing one or more keystrokes in sequence. These commands appear as follows:

Notation	Meaning
x	Press x once
dw	In sequence, press d, then w
dap	In sequence, press d, a, then p

Most of these sequences involve two or three keystrokes, but some are longer. Deciphering the meaning of Vim's Normal mode command sequences can be challenging, but you'll get better at it with practice.

---

4. https://github.com/BurntSushi/ripgrep
5. https://github.com/BurntSushi/ripgrep/releases

Playing Chords

When you see a keystroke such as `<C-p>`, it doesn't mean "Press `<`, then `C`, then `-`, and so on." The `<C-p>` notation is equivalent to `Ctrl-p`, which means "While holding down the `Ctrl` key, press the `p` key."

I didn't choose this notation without good reason. Vim's documentation uses it (:help key-notation), and we can also use it in defining custom key mappings. Some of Vim's commands are formed by combining chords and keystrokes in sequence, and this notation handles them well. Consider these examples:

Notation	Meaning
`<C-n>`	While holding `Ctrl` press `n`
`g<C-]>`	Press `g`, then while holding `Ctrl` press `]`
`<C-r>0`	While holding `Ctrl` press `r`, then release `Ctrl` and press `0`
`<C-w><C-=>`	While holding `Ctrl` press `w` then `=`

Placeholders

Many of Vim's commands require two or more keystrokes to be entered in sequence. Some commands must be followed by a particular kind of keystroke, while other commands can be followed by any key on the keyboard. I use curly braces to denote the set of valid keystrokes that can follow a command. Here are some examples:

Notation	Meaning
`f{char}`	Press `f`, followed by any other character
`` `{a-z} ``	Press `` ` ``, followed by any lowercase letter
`m{a-zA-Z}`	Press `m`, followed by any lowercase or uppercase letter
`d{motion}`	Press `d`, followed by any motion command
`<C-r>{register}`	While holding `Ctrl` press `r`, then release `Ctrl` and press the address of a register
`<C-v>{nondigit}`	While holding `Ctrl` press `v`, then release `Ctrl` and press any nondigit key

Showing Special Keys

Some keys are called by name. This table shows a selection of them:

Notation	Meaning
<Esc>	Press the Escape key
<CR>	Press the carriage return key (also known as <Enter>)
<Tab>	Press the Tab key
<S-Tab>	While holding Shift press <Tab>
<M-j>	While holding Meta press j
<Up>	Press the up arrow key
<Down>	Press the down arrow key
<Space>	Press the space bar
<Leader>g	In sequence, press <Leader> then g

Note that the Meta key goes by other names such as Alt and Option.

The Leader Key

The <Leader> key can be customized to suit your preference. The default <Leader> key is \, but lots of people prefer to set it to the , key. You can set the leader key by putting this in your vimrc file:

```
let mapleader = ','
```

When you see the <Leader>g notation, you can translate the meaning to ,g, or \g, or whatever is appropriate for your configuration.

Interacting with the Command Line

In some tips you'll execute a command line, either in a shell or from inside Vim. For example, you might be instructed to change to a directory from the provided source code examples, before opening a particular file. The $ prompt in these examples indicates that the commands are to be run in an external shell:

```
⇒ $ cd code/terminal/
⇒ $ nvim readme.md
```

Inside of Vim, pressing the : key switches from Normal mode to Command-Line mode. In this mode, you can type out Ex commands such as :write and :quit, using the <CR> key to execute the command. In the following examples, the : prompt indicates that the commands are to be executed using Vim's Command-Line mode:

⟹ `:s/cool/awesome/g`
⟹ `:write`

Any time you see an Ex command listed inline, such as :write, assume that the <CR> key is pressed to execute the command. Nothing happens otherwise, so consider <CR> to be implicit.

In Neovim, you can run a shell inside of a terminal buffer using the :terminal command. (This is covered in detail in Chapter 5, *Neovim's Built-In Terminal Emulator*, on page 69.) In the following examples, the » prompt indicates that the commands are to be executed in a shell within a terminal buffer:

⟹ `» cat readme.md`
⟹ `» top`

This table summarizes the meaning of these different prompts:

Prompt	Meaning
:	Use Command-Line mode to execute an Ex command
$	Enter the command line in an external shell
»	Enter the command line in an internal shell (within a terminal buffer)

Minimal Configuration

To follow the examples in this book, you'll need to make sure that 'nocompatible' is set and that filetype detection is enabled. Prior to version 8 of Vim, you had to specify these settings in your vimrc file:

```
set nocompatible
filetype plugin indent on
```

With the release of Vim 8, these are now default settings (:help defaults.vim). That means you don't have to include those lines in your vimrc, unless you want to keep your configuration backward compatible with older versions of Vim. You can check that filetype detection is enabled by running:

⟹ `:filetype`
‹ `filetype detection:ON  plugin:ON  indent:ON`

Make sure that you can see detection:ON, otherwise you'll have trouble following some of the tips in this book.

Using Factory Settings

Some of the tips in *Modern Vim* are written on the assumption that you're running Vim with the "factory settings." If you want to follow the steps in these tips, you can do so by temporarily moving your Vim configuration to a

location where it will be ignored when you start up your editor. For example,
you could rename your Vim 8 configuration files like this:

```
$ mv ~/.vim ~/.xvim
$ mv ~/.vimrc ~/.xvimrc
$ mkdir ~/.vim
```

After following the tip, you can restore your Vim configuration by moving the
files back to their original locations:

```
$ rm -r ~/.vim
$ mv ~/.xvim ~/.vim
$ mv ~/.xvimrc ~/.vimrc
```

For Neovim, you could switch to the factory settings by running:

```
$ mv ~/.config/nvim ~/.config/xnvim
$ mkdir ~/.config/nvim
```

Then you could switch back again by running:

```
$ rm -r ~/.config/nvim
$ mv ~/.config/xnvim ~/.config/nvim
```

Downloading the Examples

The examples in *Modern Vim* usually begin by showing the contents of a file
before we change it. These code listings will include a file path that will look
similar to the following:

green-bottles.txt
```
10 green bottles hanging on the wall.
```

Each time you see a file listed with its file path in this manner, it means you
can download the example. I recommend that you open the file in Vim and
try out the exercises for yourself. It's the best way to learn!

To follow along, download the examples and source code[6] from the *Modern
Vim* book page at The Pragmatic Bookshelf,[7] which is where you will also find
a place to post any errata. If you're reading on an electronic device that's
connected to the Internet, you can also fetch each file one by one by clicking
the filename. Try it with the previous example.

Now, let's get started!

---

6. https://pragprog.com/titles/modvim/source_code
7. https://pragprog.com/titles/modvim

CHAPTER 1

Get Modern Vim

If you want to use the features described in this book, you'll need to install a *modern* Vim. You have three choices: use Vim 8, use Neovim, or use both.

Upgrade to Vim 8

Vim is ubiquitous. It runs on most computers, and many systems have Vim installed by default. Knowing Vim is a skill set you can take with you wherever you go, and for many people, that's Vim's killer feature.

As an open source project, Vim is in good health.[1] Bug fixes and new features are being developed continuously. On many systems, the version of Vim that's installed by default is out of date, but you can enjoy the latest features by upgrading to Vim 8.

Switch to Neovim

Neovim is a fork of Vim. Its main goal to make the editor more *hackable* has been achieved by modernizing the codebase, introducing a new plugin architecture, and sharing responsibility for the codebase with the community.

The Neovim community has done a great deal of work to refactor Vim's codebase, making it simpler and more maintainable. It works diligently to merge patches from upstream Vim, so that bug fixes and features developed for Vim 8 eventually make their way into Neovim.

Neovim's remote plugin architecture allows you to extend the editor by making remote procedure calls (RPCs) using any programming language. At the same time, Vim script still works in Neovim, so most plugins written for Vim also work in Neovim.

---

1. https://github.com/vim/vim

Vim's development is discussed via a mailing list, while Neovim's development happens on GitHub. I follow the development of both projects with interest, but I find Neovim's community and development model to be more approachable. I've never submitted a patch to Vim, but I've had several patches for Neovim accepted.

Use Both

You can use Vim and Neovim side by side, so you don't have to use either one exclusively. If you like, you can set them up so that both editors use the same configuration files and plugins. I switched to using Neovim as my main development editor a couple of years ago, and I have no regrets. When I'm working on another computer where Neovim isn't available, I'm happy to use Vim instead.

Vim and Neovim each have their place, and I expect both projects to thrive for many years to come.

Tip 1

Installing Vim 8

 Vim 8 only

You probably have Vim installed on your system, but you may not have the latest version. In this tip, you'll get some pointers on how to install version 8 of Vim.

You can find out which version of Vim you have installed using the --version flag. This excerpt shows the version currently installed on my Mac:

```
$ vim --version
VIM - Vi IMproved 8.0 (2016 Sep 12, compiled Aug 15 2017 05:26:25)
MacOS X (unix) version
Included patches: 1-946
Huge version without GUI.  Features included (+) or not (-):
+acl              +file_in_path    +mouse_sgr       +tag_old_static
+arabic           +find_in_path    -mouse_sysmouse  -tag_any_white
+autocmd          +float           +mouse_urxvt     -tcl
...
```

The first line shows that this is version 8.0, and you can also see which features have been enabled in your build of Vim. You want to make sure that your build has the +job, +channel, +timers, and +packages features enabled.

If you're on an older version of Vim, you'll need to upgrade. You could download a prebuilt binary using your package manager, or you could download the source code from GitHub and build it yourself. Following are instructions for installing Vim on Debian and macOS.

Installing Vim 8 on Linux

Linux users should be able to get Vim with their package manager. For example, on Debian, you'd install Vim by running:

```
$ sudo apt-get install vim
```

If you're still on version 7 after running that command, then you'll need to install the Personal Package Archive (PPA):

```
$ sudo add-apt-repository ppa:jonathonf/vim
$ sudo apt update
$ sudo apt install vim
```

Installing Vim 8 on macOS

On macOS, you can install Vim using Homebrew:

```
$ brew install vim
```

If you previously used Homebrew to install an older version of Vim, then you'll want to run this instead:

```
$ brew upgrade vim
```

Contextual Instructions for Vim

Throughout this book, you'll come across generalized instructions that look like this:

```
$ mkdir -p $VIMCONFIG/pack/bundle/start
$ mkdir -p $VIMDATA/undo
```

When running Vim on Unix, you could execute those commands by running:

```
$ mkdir -p ~/.vim/pack/bundle/start
$ mkdir -p ~/.vim/undo
```

Alternatively, you could set the $VIMCONFIG and $VIMDATA variables for your shell. For example, in bash you would run:

```
$ export VIMCONFIG=~/.vim
$ export VIMDATA=~/.vim
```

Having set these variables, you could then run the mkdir -p $VIMCONFIG/pack/bundle/start and mkdir -p $VIMDATA/undo commands verbatim.

You might be wondering why there are two variables set to the same value. That's because Neovim uses different directories to store configuration and data, whereas Vim makes no such distinction.

What's Next?

After upgrading to Vim 8, your existing vimrc should continue to work just fine. You don't need to change anything, but you might choose to modernize your configuration by using the new packages feature to install your plugins. Skip ahead to Chapter 2, *Installing Plugins*, on page 11 to learn more.

Tip 2

Switching to Neovim

 Neovim only

Neovim can be used as a drop-in replacement for Vim. In this tip, you'll find out how to install Neovim on Debian and macOS, and how to make Neovim use your existing vimrc and Vim plugins. If you want to install Neovim on another system, Neovim's wiki contains comprehensive installation instructions for many systems.[2]

Installing Neovim on Linux

Linux users should be able to get Neovim with their package manager. For example, on Debian, you'd install Neovim by running:

```
$ sudo apt-get install neovim
```

If that doesn't work, you may need to install the Personal Package Archive (PPA):

```
$ sudo add-apt-repository ppa:neovim-ppa/stable
$ sudo apt-get install neovim
```

Alternatively, you can install Neovim as an AppImage,[3] which is a universal package that should work on most modern Linux distributions. You can get

---

2. https://github.com/neovim/neovim/wiki/Installing-Neovim
3. http://appimage.org

The Origins of Neovim

In 2014, when version 7.4 of Vim was current, Thiago de Arruda submitted a patch that introduced multi-threading capabilities to Vim. The patch wasn't accepted, and he didn't receive any feedback to suggest why the contribution was rejected. In response, Thiago created a fork of Vim and named it *Neovim.* To support his work on this project, Thiago ran a fundraising campaign,[a] which raised over $33,000.

Thiago led the development of Neovim for 18 months and built a strong community around the project. When Thiago stepped down in late 2015, Justin Keyes stepped in as lead developer.

Today, reading the original project goals on BountySource, I'm struck by how ambitious the Neovim project was. And I'm impressed to realize that all of the project's original goals have been met.

---

a.   https://www.bountysource.com/teams/neovim/fundraiser

the latest nightly build from the Neovim releases page.[4] After downloading, you need to make the package executable:

```
$ curl -LO https://github.com/neovim/neovim/releases/download/nightly/nvim.appimage
$ chmod u+x nvim.appimage
```

You could then launch Neovim by running:

```
$ ./nvim.appimage
```

If you choose this option, you may want to set up an alias so that you can launch Neovim without typing so many characters.

Installing Neovim on macOS

On macOS, you can install Neovim using Homebrew:

```
$ brew install neovim
```

Launching Neovim

"Neovim" is the name of the software; "neovim" is the name of the package; and the executable command is abbreviated to nvim. When you've installed it, launch Neovim by running:

```
$ nvim
```

---

4.   https://github.com/neovim/neovim/releases

The act of typing "vim" is probably burned into your fingers' muscle memory. You might want to configure your shell with an alias so that typing "vim" starts Neovim instead of Vim. You could also set the $VISUAL variable to nvim, so that programs that launch a text editor (such as git commit) will use Neovim. In bash, you could set that up as follows:

```
nvim-aliases.sh
# Use Neovim as "preferred editor"
export VISUAL=nvim

# Use Neovim instead of Vim or Vi
alias vim=nvim
alias vi=nvim
```

For a couple of examples showing how $VISUAL can be useful, skip ahead to Tip 22, *Using an Existing nvim Instance as the Preferred Editor*, on page 91.

Reusing Your Vim Configuration

For a smooth transition from Vim to Neovim, it helps to reuse your existing configuration. Neovim can load your Vim runtime configuration files, but first you have to tell it where to find them.

When Vim starts up, it looks in your ~/.vim directory for a vimrc configuration file. The equivalent configuration file for Neovim is located in a ~/.config/nvim directory and is called init.vim (:help base-directories).

You'll have to create the configuration directory for Neovim:

```
$ mkdir -p ~/.config/nvim
```

Next, create and save a ~/.config/nvim/init.vim file with the following contents:

```
init.vim
set runtimepath^=~/.vim runtimepath+=~/.vim/after
let &packpath = &runtimepath
source ~/.vim/vimrc
```

Next time you launch nvim, it should load the same runtime files as vim. That means that your Vim customizations now apply to Neovim.

Vim Script Compatibility

Most Vim plugins written in Vim script should *just work*™ in Neovim. The one area where you have to be cautious is with any plugin that uses job control to perform work asynchronously. Both Vim and Neovim support this functionality, but their APIs are different. Since the job control feature is relatively new, this issue doesn't affect many plugins.

Contextual Instructions for Neovim

Throughout this book, you'll come across generalized instructions that look like this:

```
$ mkdir -p $VIMCONFIG/pack/bundle/start
$ mkdir -p $VIMDATA/undo
```

When running Neovim on Unix, you could execute those commands by running:

```
$ mkdir -p ~/.config/nvim/pack/bundle/start
$ mkdir -p ~/.local/share/nvim/undo
```

Alternatively, you could set the $VIMCONFIG and $VIMDATA variables for your shell. For example, in bash you would run:

```
$ export VIMCONFIG=~/.config/nvim
$ export VIMDATA=~/.local/share/nvim
```

Having set these variables, you could then run the mkdir -p $VIMCONFIG/pack/bundle/start and mkdir -p $VIMDATA/undo commands verbatim.

Tip 3

Enabling Python Support in Neovim

 Neovim only

In Neovim, Python is not supported out of the box. If you want to use plugins and tools that are implemented in Python (such as neovim-remote), then you'll have to install the Python client.

In Vim 8, you can have support for either Python 2 or Python 3. (You could have support for neither, but you can't have support for both!) Find out which version of Python is supported in Vim 8 by running :version and looking for +python or +python3. If your version of Vim 8 has support for Python 2, but you need Python 3, you'll have to recompile Vim.

In Neovim, however, you can enable support for both Python 2 and Python 3 at the same time. Try running this command in Neovim:

```
:py3 print('hello')
E117: Unknown function: provider#python3#Call
```

The :py3 {statement} command executes the specified statement using a Python 3 interpreter. If this doesn't work out of the box, you can fix it by setting up the Python provider.

Meet Neovim's Providers

Neovim uses *providers* to implement some features whose behavior may depend on the system and environment, such as clipboard support. Different systems have different ways of exposing their clipboard. For example, on macOS, the pbpaste and pbcopy commands allow you to get and set the clipboard; whereas on Linux, you can use either xclip or xsel to get and set the X11 clipboard. If you're running an operating system headlessly, there may not even be a system clipboard with which to interact.

In Vim 8, clipboard support has to be enabled at *compile time*. You can check if your version of Vim 8 has clipboard support by running :version and looking for the +clipboard or +xterm_clipboard features.

In Neovim, clipboard support is enabled at *runtime*. The clipboard provider checks to see if any suitable clipboard tools are available in your $PATH. If such a tool is found, the provider uses the appropriate shell commands to get and set the system clipboard. The user interface is the same in both Vim 8 and Neovim: You can use the + and * registers to interact with the system clipboard.

You can check if you have clipboard support enabled in Neovim by running :checkhealth. This runs diagnostic tests and generates a report with details for each provider. Currently, Neovim ships with providers that handle clipboard support, Python integration, and Ruby integration.

Enabling the Python 3 Provider

To enable the Python 3 provider, you need to install the Python client.[5] You can get this using pip:

```
$ pip3 install --user --upgrade neovim
```

Now restart Neovim and try running this command again:

```
:py3 print('hello')
hello
```

You'll see the hello message printed.

---

5. https://github.com/neovim/python-client

Installing neovim-remote

Neovim-remote[6] by Marco Hinz is a tool that lets you control Neovim processes remotely. It depends on the Python 3 Neovim client, so make sure you have that installed before you proceed.

Install the neovim-remote tool with `pip`:

```
$ pip3 install --user --upgrade neovim-remote
```

The package is called `neovim-remote`, but the executable is abbreviated to `nvr`. Check that it's installed okay by consulting the help:

```
$ nvr -h
usage: nvr [arguments]

Remote control Neovim instances.

...
```

For an example of how to use neovim-remote, skip ahead to Tip 21, *Avoiding Nested Neovim Instances*, on page 88.

---

6. https://github.com/mhinz/neovim-remote

CHAPTER 2

Installing Plugins

Plugins add new functionality to Vim. You'll use plugins throughout this book, so you need to be able to install them. Historically, Vim's built-in support for installing plugins has been poor, so the Vim community responded by creating plugin managers. However, since version 8, Vim's packages feature has made it easy to install plugins without relying on a plugin manager.

Tip 4

Understanding Scripts, Plugins, and Packages

Packages are a new feature in Vim 8 that make it easy to manage your plugins. To put it simply: a package is a directory that contains one or more plugins. In turn, a plugin is a directory that contains one or more scripts, and a script is a standalone file containing instructions written in Vim script.

If that all makes sense, you might want to skip to the next tip, which demonstrates how to create your own package and install plugins to it. If you're confused by this terminology, don't worry. Read this tip to get a better grip on these concepts.

Scripts Add Functionality to Vim

Vim has had basic support for scripts since version 5. A *script* is a standalone file containing instructions written in Vim script that adds new functionality to Vim. Here's a simple example script that defines a function, a command, and a Normal mode mapping:

```
hello.vim
function! SayHello()
  echo 'Hello, world!'
endfunction

command! Hello call SayHello()

nnoremap Q :Hello<CR>
```

You can load a script manually by running :source {path}, where {path} locates the script you want to run. For example, you could load the hello.vim script:

```
⇒ :source code/hello.vim
⇒ :Hello
❮ Hello, world!
```

After sourcing that script, you can use the functions, commands, and mappings that it defines. (Try pressing Q!) When Vim starts up, it looks for scripts in certain locations on disk and automatically sources them. Your vimrc file is one of the first scripts to be loaded, which makes it the ideal place to write your startup configuration.

Plugins Make It Easy to Organize and Share Scripts

If you write a script that could be useful to other Vim users, you might like to turn it into a *plugin*. That simply means creating a directory with the name you want to give your plugin, then moving your script into a plugin subdirectory within. A demo-plugin containing one script and an accompanying documentation file might look like this:

```
demo-plugin
├── doc
│   └── demo.txt
└── plugin
    └── demo.vim
```

Vim has conventions on how the subdirectories within a plugin should be named. Depending on what a plugin does, it might contain scripts within subdirectories named ftplugin, indent, syntax, among others. When a plugin is installed, Vim automatically sources the scripts it finds in these subdirectories.

Installing a plugin means adding it to Vim's 'runtimepath' (:help 'runtimepath'). You could do this by manipulating the 'runtimepath' option by hand. For example, you could install the demo-plugin to an arbitrary directory, then append that directory to Vim's 'runtimepath':

```
⇒ :set runtimepath+=$VIMCONFIG/arbitrary/demo-plugin
```

Vim has supported plugins since version 6, but until recently there was no convenient way of managing the 'runtimepath'. You had to do it by hand, or you had to install a plugin to automate the runtimepath management. With version 8, Vim released the packages feature to fill this gap.

Packages Organize and Load Your Plugins

A *package* is a directory that contains one or more plugins. By convention, you create packages within a $VIMCONFIG/pack directory. Your package should contain a subdirectory called start, which is where you install the plugins that you want to load when Vim starts up.

You can create as many packages as you like. For example, you might create one package called bundle where you install plugins written by other people. Then you might create another package called myplugins where you keep the plugins that you maintain by yourself.

When Vim launches, it searches for plugins under the $VIMCONFIG/pack/*/start/ directory. Any plugins found there are added to the 'runtimepath'. In a second pass, Vim iterates through the plugins listed in the 'runtimepath' and sources any Vim script files contained within. In practice, this means that putting a plugin within your package is all that it takes to install a plugin.

Indexing the Documentation for Installed Plugins

When you add a plugin to one of your packages, all you need to do to start using that plugin is restart Vim. But if you want to consult the documentation for a newly installed plugin, you have to do one more thing: index its documentation. You do this with the :helptags command.

Vim's documentation is written in a plaintext format that includes simple markup for defining *anchors* and *hyperlinks*. These make it possible to navigate the documentation quickly. For example, try running:

```
:help user-manual
```

That opens the documentation and shows you the table of contents for the user manual. Now try positioning your cursor on the word usr_01.txt, which is marked up as a hyperlink. Press <C-]> and you'll jump to the specified anchor. You can quickly jump back to where you came from using <C-o>. These commands make it possible to navigate Vim's documentation in much the same way you would interact with a webpage.

When you use the :helptags command, Vim parses the documentation files, builds an index of anchors, and writes them to a file called tags. You only need to run :helptags once after installing a new plugin, then Vim can use the generated tags file to look up the documentation for that plugin. If you update a plugin later, you may want to run :helptags again to ensure that the documentation is up to date.

Tip 5

Installing Plugins to Your Package

With Vim 8, the packages feature makes it easy to install plugins without having to rely on a plugin manager. You can install plugins in your package and they will be automatically loaded when Vim starts up.

Preparation

To follow the steps in this tip, you may want to temporarily disable your personal Vim configuration. That way you'll be able to reproduce the examples listed here without interference from any plugins you may have already installed. To find out how, follow the steps in *Using Factory Settings*, on page xv, which also includes instructions on how to restore your own configuration afterward.

Installing Your First Plugin

First, launch Vim and inspect the 'runtimepath':

```
:echo join(split(&runtimepath, ','), "\n")
/Users/drew/.vim
/usr/local/share/vim/vimfiles
/usr/local/share/vim/vim80
/usr/local/share/vim/vimfiles/after
/Users/drew/.vim/after
```

These are Vim's default configuration directories. When you install a plugin, you want to add that plugin's directory to your 'runtimepath'.

Exit Vim and create a new directory where you'll install the plugin:

```
$ mkdir -p $VIMCONFIG/pack/bundle/start
```

The pack and start directories have special meaning to Vim, so they have to be named like that. The bundle directory represents the package itself, and you could name it any way you like.

Now, change to that directory and clone the Git repository for vim-unimpaired:

```
$ cd $VIMCONFIG/pack/bundle/start
$ git clone https://github.com/tpope/vim-unimpaired.git
```

Relaunch Vim and inspect the 'runtimepath' again:

```
:echo join(split(&runtimepath, ','), "\n")
/Users/drew/.vim
/Users/drew/.vim/pack/bundle/start/vim-unimpaired
/usr/local/share/vim/vimfiles
...
```

In addition to the default directories, the 'runtimepath' now includes the vim-unimpaired directory. That means you can use the mappings supplied by the unimpaired plugin. Try running the =on command to toggle line numbering on and off.

Note that if you were to install a new plugin to the start directory while Vim is running, you wouldn't be able to use that plugin right away. Restarting Vim would cause the new plugin to be added to the 'runtimepath' making it available for use.

There are various reasons why you might hesitate to restart Vim. Perhaps you've set your workspace up just the way you need it and you don't want to lose that context. If that's a concern, check out Chapter 6, *Sessions*, on page 95, which describes a mechanism that allows you to save your Vim session then restore it later.

Indexing the Documentation

You can use the features from the unimpaired plugin, but there's something missing: documentation. Try looking up the help page and you'll draw a blank:

```
:help unimpaired
E149: Sorry, no help for unimpaired
```

The unimpaired plugin includes documentation, but Vim doesn't yet know where to find the appropriate file. You can fix this by running the :helptags ALL command (:help :helptags):

```
:helptags ALL
:help unimpaired
```

(You may see an error message like this: E152: Cannot open {dir} for writing. If that happens, it means you don't have write permissions for at least one of the directories in your runtimepath. Despite this noisy warning, the command should still succeed in all of the directories where you do have write permissions, so there's nothing to worry about. You can suppress the error message by running :silent helptags ALL.)

This time, when you look up the help page for unimpaired, Vim takes you to the documentation. You only need to run :helptags once after installing (or updating) a plugin.

Installing an Optional Plugin

Some plugins are for everyday use, while others may come in handy only occasionally. Vim's packages can contain optional plugins, which you can load when needed. Let's install the Scriptease plugin[1] this way. This plugin provides extra functionality that is useful when developing Vim script files.

Start by creating an opt subdirectory in the bundle package, and then clone the plugin to that directory:

```
$ mkdir -p $VIMCONFIG/pack/bundle/opt
$ cd $VIMCONFIG/pack/bundle/opt
$ git clone https://github.com/tpope/vim-scriptease.git
```

If you launch Vim and inspect the 'runtimepath', you won't find anything new:

```
:echo join(split(&runtimepath, ','), "\n")
/Users/drew/.vim
/Users/drew/.vim/pack/bundle/start/vim-unimpaired
/usr/local/share/vim/vimfiles
...
```

By default, our optional plugin is not loaded. Use the :packadd command to activate the plugin (:help :packadd):

```
:packadd vim-scriptease
```

If you inspect the 'runtimepath' now, you should find the Scriptease plugin installed:

```
:echo join(split(&runtimepath, ','), "\n")
/Users/drew/.vim
/Users/drew/.vim/pack/bundle/opt/vim-scriptease
/Users/drew/.vim/pack/bundle/start/vim-unimpaired
...
```

---

1. https://github.com/tpope/vim-scriptease

And you can use the features it provides. Try running the :scriptnames command to see for yourself. Having loaded the plugin with :packadd, it'll be available until Vim quits. Next time you launch Vim, the optional plugin won't be loaded.

If you want to consult the documentation for a newly installed optional plugin, you'll have to run the :helptags command to index that plugin's documentation.

Updating Plugins in Your Package

Plugins, like all software, are never complete. There will be bug fixes, new features, and general improvements. If you want to run the latest version of a plugin, you'll need to update it from time to time.

Installing plugins with Git means that you can easily update to the latest version by running git pull:

```
$ cd $VIMCONFIG/pack/bundle/start/vim-unimpaired
$ git pull
$ cd $VIMCONFIG/pack/bundle/opt/vim-scriptease
$ git pull
```

As you install more plugins, the prospect of doing this by hand for each plugin becomes unappealing. You could automate the process by writing a shell script. Alternatively, you could install a Vim plugin that takes care of this, as demonstrated in Tip 6, *Managing Plugins with minpac*, on page 18.

Migrating to Vim Packages

Now that you've reached the end of this tip, you can discard the temporary Vim configuration you created:

```
$ rm -rf $VIMCONFIG
```

Refer back to *Using Factory Settings*, on page xv for instructions on how to restore your own personal configuration.

Prior to version 8, Vim's built-in support for installing plugins was sorely lacking. Tim Pope wrote the Pathogen plugin[2] to ease the pain of managing your 'runtimepath'. Vim's packages feature implements similar functionality to Pathogen, but it has the advantage of being built-in.

Pathogen works fine with Vim 8, so there's no urgent need to migrate away from it. If you'd like to switch to using Vim's built-in packages, migrate by running these commands:

---

2.   https://github.com/tpope/vim-pathogen

```
$ mkdir -p $VIMCONFIG/pack/bundle/{start,opt}
$ mv $VIMCONFIG/bundle/* $VIMCONFIG/pack/bundle/start/
$ rm $VIMCONFIG/autoload/pathogen.vim
```

You'll also want to remove the line execute pathogen#infect() from your .vimrc file.

Tip 6

Managing Plugins with minpac

minpac is a minimal plugin manager that builds on top of Vim's new packages feature. With minpac, you can easily install plugins, keep them up to date, and uninstall them. In this tip, you'll learn how to install and configure minpac.

Preparation

If you're currently using a plugin manager such as Vundle[3] or vim-plug,[4] you will have to temporarily disable it so that you can follow the steps in this tip. To find out how, see *Using Factory Settings*, on page xv, which also includes instructions on how to restore your own configuration afterward.

Installing minpac

minpac should be installed as an optional plugin. Let's create a new package, which will contain the plugins that you'll manage using minpac. Name it after the plugin itself:

```
$ mkdir -p $VIMCONFIG/pack/minpac/opt
```

Next, add the minpac repository to the opt directory:

```
$ cd $VIMCONFIG/pack/minpac/opt
$ git clone https://github.com/k-takata/minpac.git
```

Now, open up the ~/.vimrc file and append these two lines to load and initialize the plugin:

```
packadd minpac
call minpac#init()
```

Save the .vimrc, then reload it and inspect the runtimepath:

---

3.   https://github.com/VundleVim/Vundle.vim
4.   https://github.com/junegunn/vim-plug

```
⇒ :write
⇒ :source %
⇒ :echo join(split(&runtimepath, ','), "\n")
❮ /Users/drew/.vim
  /Users/drew/.vim/pack/minpac/opt/minpac
  ...
```

There! You've successfully installed minpac.

Adding and Updating Plugins with minpac

To register plugins with your minpac package, you would call the minpac#add()
function. As its first argument, this function takes a string made up of two
parts separated with a slash (/): the plugin author's GitHub username, followed by the name of the plugin. This function can also take an optional
second argument, which is a dictionary of configuration options.

Append these lines to your ~/.vimrc:

```
call minpac#add('tpope/vim-unimpaired')
call minpac#add('tpope/vim-scriptease', {'type': 'opt'})
```

By default, minpac installs plugins to the start directory, but to install an
optional plugin you need to specify {'type': 'opt'} as the second argument.

Now to execute these calls, save your ~/.vimrc and reload it:

```
⇒ :write
⇒ :source %
```

And finally, invoke the minpac#update() function:

```
⇒ :call minpac#update()
❮ All plugins are up to date. (Updated: 0, Newly installed: 2)
```

For each registered plugin, minpac#update() fetches the repository from GitHub.
Newly added plugins will be installed fresh, and existing plugins will be
updated. After fetching plugins, minpac runs the :helptags command to ensure
all documentation is up to date.

As minpac handles each plugin, it echoes a message. These usually go by too
quickly to read, but if you want to review them afterward, run the following:

```
⇒ :messages
❮ Installed: vim-scriptease
  Installed: vim-unimpaired
  All plugins are up to date. (Updated: 0, Newly installed: 2)
```

Messages are only printed when a plugin is updated or newly installed. If you call the `minpac#update()` function a second time, you'll only see one message: "All plugins are up to date." (Unless it's your lucky day and Tim Pope has just updated one of those plugins!)

Note that minpac uses Vim's jobs API to fetch plugins in parallel.

The `minpac#update()` function has downloaded these plugins onto your file system, but newly installed plugins are not present in your 'runtimepath' so you can't use them yet. The quickest way to fix this is to restart Vim.

You can make minpac manage itself by adding this line to your vimrc:

```
call minpac#add('k-takata/minpac', {'type': 'opt'})
```

If a new release of the minpac plugin comes out, you can upgrade to the latest version by running :call minpac#update(). This won't happen often because minpac is stable, but it's a nice touch all the same.

Removing Plugins with minpac

minpac also makes it easy to uninstall plugins with the `minpac#clean()` function.

Remove this line from your ~/.vimrc file:

```
call minpac#add('tpope/vim-scriptease', {'type': 'opt'})
```

Then save and reload:

⇒ `:write`
⇒ `:source %`

Now, invoke the clean() function:

⇒ `:call minpac#clean()`
‹ `/Users/drew/.vim/pack/minpac/opt/vim-scriptease`
`Removing the above directory. [y/N]?`

You're presented with a prompt. Pressing y causes the vim-scriptease directory to be removed.

Creating Commands

It's rather a lot to type out :call minpac#update() every time you want to update your plugins. Add convenience by creating your own custom commands:

```
command! PackUpdate call minpac#update()
command! PackClean call minpac#clean()
```

Append these lines to your ~/.vimrc file, then save and reload it.

Let's try them out:

⇒ `:PackUpdate`
‹ `All plugins are up to date.`
⇒ `:PackClean`
‹ `Already clean.`

A Modern and Minimal Plugin Manager

Plugin managers such as Vundle and vim-plug pre-date the packages functionality that came out in version 8 of Vim. These plugins had to invent their own solutions for managing the runtimepath, whereas minpac simply builds on top of the packages feature and gets the runtimepath management for free. minpac can install and update plugins in parallel. This is made possible by Vim's job control feature (:help channel), which is also new in version 8. (For Neovim, look up :help job-control.)

By building on top of native functionality, minpac is able to provide the basic features of a plugin manager with a minimal codebase. However, it may not offer all the features mature plugin managers do. If minpac meets all of your needs, I encourage you to try it out.

CHAPTER 3

Opening Files

Opening files is one of the most common tasks you perform when coding. Vim's built-in functionality gives you basic commands for opening any readable file by specifying its filepath. Tab-completion can save you from typing every character of a filepath, but you may still end up using a lot of keystrokes to locate the file you want. In this chapter, you'll learn about a few different techniques for opening files with less effort.

Tip 7

Finding Files Using Fuzzy Path Matching

You can rely on Vim's built-in :edit {filepath} command for opening any file on your file system, but specifying a filepath can require a lot of typing. Using a fuzzy finder can usually produce the same result with far fewer keystrokes.

Preparation

Vim users are spoiled for choice when it comes to fuzzy finder plugins. In this tip, you'll be using Junegunn Choi's excellent fzf tool.[1] This consists of two parts: a standalone fzf program, which you can run in your shell, and a Vim plugin, which depends upon the external program.

Installing and Configuring fzf

You can install the fzf repository to your bundle package like this:

1. https://github.com/junegunn/fzf

⇒ `$ cd $VIMCONFIG/pack/bundle/start`
⇒ `$ git clone https://github.com/junegunn/fzf`

Not only does this repository include a simple Vim plugin (which you've now installed), but it also contains source code for building the fzf executable. Run this command to install the executable in the repository's bin directory:

⇒ `$ $VIMCONFIG/pack/bundle/start/fzf/install --bin`

You'll need to make sure that the bin directory is in your $PATH. Add this line to the startup script for your shell (e.g., ~/.bashrc if you're using bash):

```
export PATH=$PATH:$VIMCONFIG/pack/bundle/start/fzf/bin
```

Source that startup script (or open a new shell), and you should now be able to run the fzf executable:

⇒ `$ fzf --help`

Next, start a new instance of Vim and you should be able to run the :FZF command:

⇒ `:FZF`

That opens the fzf picker interface. You'll find out how to use it shortly, but for now you can dismiss the fzf picker by pressing `<C-c>`.

For convenience, I'd suggest creating a Normal mode mapping by adding this line to your vimrc file:

fzf-mappings.vim
```
nnoremap <C-p> :<C-u>FZF<CR>
```

After sourcing your vimrc file, you can invoke the fzf file finder by pressing `<C-p>`.

Exploring the Demo Project

The source code that accompanies this book includes a big-docs directory. Here's a small portion of the file listing:

```
big-docs
├── app
│     ├── components
│     │     └── table-of-contents.js
│     ├── templates
│     │     └── components
│     │           └── table-of-contents.hbs
│     └── styles
│           └── components
│                 └── _toc.scss
```

```
└── tests
    └── integration
        └── components
            └── table-of-contents-test.js
```

The big-docs project contains many more files and subdirectories, but you'll be focusing on these in the examples that follow.

Opening Files by Specifying Their Filepath

First we'll look at opening files by specifying their filepath. Change to the big-docs directory and open Vim:

```
$ cd code/big-docs
$ vim
```

Suppose you want to open the table-of-contents.js and table-of-contents.hbs files in two splits. You could use these commands:

```
:edit app/components/table-of-contents.js
:vsplit app/templates/components/table-of-contents.hbs
```

That might look like a lot of typing, but <Tab> completion can do most of the work for you. To produce these commands, you can get away with typing as little as this:

```
:e a<Tab>com<Tab>t<Tab>
:vs a<Tab>t<Tab>co<Tab>t<Tab>
```

Even so, that's still a lot of keystrokes. In projects like this, where the files are organized with several levels of subdirectories, specifying the complete filepath can be a bit of a drag. If you want to get the same result with fewer keystrokes, try fuzzy matching.

Opening Files by Fuzzy-Matching Their Filepath

Give yourself a blank slate by restarting Vim in the big-docs directory:

```
$ cd code/big-docs
$ vim
```

This time you're going to use fzf to open the table-of-contents.js file. Invoke the fuzzy finder interface by typing :FZF or using the <C-p> mapping you created earlier. At the prompt that appears, type the characters tocj then press the <CR> key:

```
/tocj<CR>
```

Boom! You're there!

Now, use the same technique to open the table-of-contents.hbs file. This time, type toch and press <C-v> to open the selected file in a vertical split:

⇒ `/toch<C-v>`

Counting keystrokes, there's no contest: fzf gets you the file you want much more quickly than the built-in :edit command.

How Does Fuzzy Matching Work?

When you launch the fuzzy finder, it starts off with a list of filepaths for every file beneath your current working directory. You can filter that list by providing a query. When you type "t" at the prompt, the list is filtered to only include filepaths containing that letter. With the query "to," the list is filtered to only include filepaths containing the letter "t" followed by the letter "o." Those letters have to appear in that order, but they don't have to be adjacent to each other. That's what makes this a fuzzy match.

As well as *filtering* the list of matches, the fuzzy finder also *sorts* the results using a ranking algorithm. The more characters you include in your query, the shorter the list of matches becomes. If you craft your query carefully, then the file you want to select will surface at the top of the list of matches.

In the following table, you can see the top-ranked matches for a handful of example queries. I suggest you spend some time studying this table and looking for patterns:

Query	Ranked Matches
toc	1. app/styles/components/_toc.scss
	2. app/components/table-of-contents.js
	3. app/templates/components/table-of-contents.hbs
	4. tests/integration/components/table-of-contents-test.js
tocj	1. app/components/table-of-contents.js
	2. tests/integration/components/table-of-contents-test.js
toct	1. tests/integration/components/table-of-contents-test.js
	2. app/components/table-of-contents.js
toch	1. app/templates/components/table-of-contents.hbs

Note that for the query toct, the first match highlights the first letter of "test" even though there are two "t"s in the word "contents" before it. Letters appearing at the start of a word get a higher score than those that appear later in a word. Even if that explanation sounds complicated, the results feel quite intuitive, so don't think too hard about it!

In the previous examples, I constructed queries that are deliberately terse. These sample queries happen to work for this particular set of files, but that doesn't mean they are the correct answers. Any query that locates your target file will do. If you wanted to open the table-of-contents-test.js file, any of these queries would work: testtabcon, tacotest, toct. You don't win a trophy for constructing a shorter query than your coworkers.

If you want some practice, try using the fuzzy finder to open these files in the big-docs directory:

- app/styles/components/_footer.scss
- app/routes/project-version/namespaces/namespace/index.js
- app/controllers/project-version/namespaces/namespace/properties.js
- tests/integration/components/search-input/dropdown-header-test.js

Or better still: Try using the fuzzy finder on your own projects.

Operating the fzf Interface

You've got two basic strategies for selecting a file in the fzf interface. The first is to keep refining your query until your target file is the topmost result, which is selected by default. The other strategy is to specify just enough of a query so that your target file appears near the top of the list, then use <C-k> and <C-j> to change the selection.

For example, suppose you want to open the table-of-contents-test.js file. You invoke :FZF and enter the query toc. That filters the list and your target file is the fourth match. At this point, you could press the <C-k> repeatedly until you've selected your target file. Or you could refine the query to toct, which would make your target file the topmost result.

The <CR> key triggers the default action on the selected item in the fzf interface. In this case, that means opening the file in the current window. You can use <C-x>, <C-v>, or <C-t> respectively, to open the file in a horizontal split, a vertical split, or a new tab page.

The table on page 28 summarizes some of the most useful keys that you can use to operate the fzf interface.

Command	Effect
{alphanum}	Refine the query
<C-j>	Select previous item from matchlist
<C-k>	Select next item from matchlist
<CR>	Open the selected file in the current window
<C-x>	Open the selected file in a horizontal split
<C-v>	Open the selected file in a vertical split
<C-t>	Open the selected file in a new tab page
<C-c>	Dismiss the fzf picker

Filtering Out Files

By default, fzf builds a list of all the files beneath your current working directory. It generates that list of files using a variation of the find . -type f command.
You can count the number of files in the big-docs directory like this:

```
$ cd code/big-docs
$ find . -type f | wc -l
191
```

Rounding up, that's about 200 files. Now, let's make things a bit more busy
by installing the project's dependencies:

```
$ npm install
$ find . -type f | wc -l
9925
```

The npm install command downloads libraries into the node_modules directory,
resulting in thousands of extra files. If you launch Vim now and invoke the
:FZF command, you'll find many more matches for your queries. That adds a
lot of noise and makes it harder to find the file you're looking for. Try using
indexjs as a query and you'll see what I mean.

It would be helpful if you could exclude all files beneath node_modules from the
list that's passed to fzf. A common strategy here is to build a list containing
only the files that are under version control. Turn the big-docs directory into a
Git repository by running these commands:

```
$ git init
$ echo "node_modules/" >> .gitignore
$ git add .
$ git commit -m "Initialize"
```

The echo command creates a .gitignore file, instructing Git to ignore everything in the node_modules directory. Now you can use the git ls-files command to list all the files that are under version control:

```
$ git ls-files | wc -l
175
```

By setting the FZF_DEFAULT_COMMAND environment variable, you can specify how fzf should build a list of files. Try setting it like this:

```
export FZF_DEFAULT_COMMAND='git ls-files'
```

Now when you launch fzf, it will exclude all of the files from node_modules. That makes it much easier to find the files in your project.

One thing to watch out for is that git ls-files only lists files that Git knows about. Suppose that you've just created new-file.txt within your Git repository. That file won't be listed by the git ls-files command until you run git add new-file.txt. This leads to a situation where fzf won't show you files that you've just created, which can be confusing.

Of course, there's another downside to using git ls-files: it's useless outside of a Git repository! For a more flexible solution, I recommend using Ripgrep (see *Other Software Requirements*, on page xi):

```
export FZF_DEFAULT_COMMAND='rg --files'
```

The rg --files command is able to filter out files that are marked ignore in Git, Mercurial, and Subversion repositories. When used in a Git repository, this command does include files that have yet to be added to the Git index. When used outside of a version control repository, it falls back to listing all files.

Fuzzy Finding Other Sources

What if you want to select a buffer from the buffer list? Normally you'd do that using the built-in :buffer {bufname} command (:help :buffer). But wouldn't it be cool if you could invoke your fuzzy finder on the list of open buffers?

Or suppose you want to re-run an Ex command from your history. Normally you'd do that by pressing : to switch to Command-Line mode, then using <Up> / <Down> to scroll through your history until you find the command you want to repeat (:help c_Up). Alternatively, imagine if you could invoke your fuzzy finder on your command history, typing a query to filter the list, then executing the selected match.

You can feed fzf a list, have it filter the results based on a query, then perform an action with the selected result. In fzf terminology, the list of items to be filtered is called the *source*, and the action to be performed on the selected result is called the *sink*. You could provide the buffer list as a source, and make opening the selected buffer be the sink. Or you could provide the command history as a source, and make executing the selected command be the sink.

If you're excited by the idea of using fzf with various different sources, you should check out the fzf.vim plugin, also by Junegunn Choi.[2] This plugin provides fuzzy matchers for a variety of sources, including the buffer list, command history, search history, helptags, and many more.

If you're using fzf only for opening files from your file system, you just need the basic fzf plugin. If you want to use fzf to do other things, like selecting a buffer or re-running an Ex command from your history, you should install the fzf.vim plugin as well. If you have ideas for fuzzy matchers that aren't already implemented in fzf.vim, then you can try rolling your own matchers using Vim script functions fzf#run() and fzf#wrap().

Tip 8

Finding Files Semantically

In a well-organized codebase, you can expect files of certain types to be located in a particular subdirectory. You may also expect related files (such as unit tests) to be found in a predictable location relative to the name and path of the file you're editing. With the Projectionist plugin, you can easily open files by category and effortlessly jump to any related files.

Preparation

In this tip, you'll use the Projectionist plugin[3] by Tim Pope. Install it to your bundle package like this:

```
$ cd $VIMCONFIG/pack/bundle/start
$ git clone https://github.com/tpope/vim-projectionist.git
```

---

2. https://github.com/junegunn/fzf.vim
3. https://github.com/tpope/vim-projectionist

Exploring the Demo Projects

The source code that accompanies this book includes two examples of a skeleton blogging application. Each example contains the same set of files, but they differ in their naming conventions.

The blog-classic application arranges files between app/adapters, app/models, and app/serializers directories. Within this directory tree, there are three files named comment.js, and you can discern what role each of those files has by looking at the name of its parent directory:

```
blog-classic
├── .projections.json
└── app
    ├── app.js
    ├── adapters
    │   ├── comment.js
    │   └── post.js
    ├── models
    │   ├── author.js
    │   ├── comment.js
    │   └── post.js
    └── serializers
        ├── comment.js
        └── post.js
```

The blog-modular application takes a different approach. The files are arranged between models/author, models/comment, and models/post directories. Within this directory tree, there are three files named model.js, and you can find out which domain object each file represents by looking at the name of its parent directory:

```
blog-modular
├── .projections.json
└── src
    ├── data
    │   └── models
    │       ├── author
    │       │   └── model.js
    │       ├── comment
    │       │   ├── adapter.js
    │       │   ├── model.js
    │       │   └── serializer.js
    │       └── post
    │           ├── adapter.js
    │           ├── model.js
    │           └── serializer.js
    └── main.js
```

Both of these applications are laid out logically according to their own conventions. If you are a developer working on applications in the real world, you might encounter projects that follow either of these layouts, or yet another layout again.

Suppose your job requires you to maintain both of these applications. Each time you switch from one codebase to another, you're going to have to rewire your thinking to match the directory layout. If you want to open the file representing a CommentModel, you need to know whether to look for model/comment.js or comment/model.js.

Those kinds of context switches can leave you feeling disoriented in a codebase, even when that codebase is well organized by its own internal logic. Wouldn't it be neat if you could just think, "open the comment model," and Vim would know where on the file system to look for it? That's where Projectionist's navigation commands come to the rescue.

Defining Navigation Commands

The Projectionist plugin makes it easy to define navigation commands. You'll soon see how these commands work, but first let's look at how to configure these commands. Projectionist uses a simple JSON format for configuration.

Each of the sample applications contains a hidden .projections.json file in the project's root directory. Open both of these files in Vim using the -O flag so that each file opens in its own window:

```
$ cd code
$ vim -O blog-{classic,modular}/.projections.json
```

You can switch between the windows using <C-w>w.

Here's an excerpt from the blog-classic/.projections.json file:

```
{
  "app/models/*.js": { "type": "model" }
}
```

To understand this we'll start on the inside and work our way out. {"type": "model"} defines a model type, which will be assigned to any file that matches the glob: app/models/*.js.

The blog-modular/.projections.json file contains a similar directive with a different glob:

```
{
  "src/data/models/*/model.js": { "type": "model" }
}
```

The Projectionist plugin detects and parses the hidden .projections.json files, defining navigation commands for each declared type. You can use the model navigation command to open the CommentModel like this:

⇒ `:Emodel comment`

The killer feature of these navigation commands is that they work contextually. If the active window contains a file from the blog-classic project, then :Emodel comment opens the app/models/comment.js file. Whereas, if the active window contains a file from the blog-modular project, that same navigation command instead opens the src/data/models/comment/model.js file.

The .projections.json files provided define navigation commands for adapters, serializers, and a main file. Here's the full listing for the blog-classic project:

blog-classic/.projections.json
```
{
  "app/app.js": { "type": "main" },
  "app/models/*.js": { "type": "model" },
  "app/adapters/*.js": { "type": "adapter" },
  "app/serializers/*.js": { "type": "serializer" }
}
```

Try running these commands from both sample projects:

⇒ `:Emain`
⇒ `:Eadapter post`
⇒ `:Emodel author`
⇒ `:Eserializer comment`

Note that the main type maps to a filepath, whereas the adapter, model, and serializer types all use a glob. The :Emain navigation command doesn't require any arguments, whereas the other navigation commands do require an argument to fill in the wildcard.

Validate Your Projections

If your .projections.json configuration file contains invalid JSON, the Projectionist plugin may start failing in a cryptic fashion, but it won't report any errors. As a human, it's all too easy to write poorly formed JSON. You might omit a vital comma or accidentally duplicate a key, and the next thing you know, you've broken your Projectionist navigation commands. That's a tricky problem to fix.

It's a good idea to run your Projectionist configuration through a JSON linter. I'd recommend using the ALE plugin, covered in Tip 12, *Linting the Current File*, on page 50, which can be configured to work with a few different linting tools that work with JSON.

Navigation Command Variations

You've already seen that the Projectionist plugin creates navigation commands that begin with a capital "E." It also creates variations of this command, beginning with capital "S", "V", and "T." The following table summarizes how these commands behave:

Command	Effect
:Etype	Opens the specified type in the current window
:Stype	Opens the specified type in a horizontal split
:Vtype	Opens the specified type in a vertical split
:Ttype	Opens the specified type in a new tabpage

To get a feel for how these work, try running these commands:

```
:Tmain
:Vmodel comment
:Sadapter comment
:Eserializer comment
```

Smart Tab Completion

You can use the `<Tab>` key to fill out your navigation commands quickly. For example, if you want to run this command:

```
:Eserializer comment
```

you can type :Es<Tab> c<Tab> instead of typing out the entire command. If there's more than one way of expanding the text you entered, then you can repeat `<Tab>` to cycle through match candidates.

When using tab completion, you can use a * character as a wildcard. For example, if you type :Emodel *nt<Tab>, the tab completion expands *nt to comment.

The tab completion behavior is a built-in Vim feature Projectionist leverages. If you want to tweak the way it works, just configure the 'wildmode' and 'wildmenu' options.

Use the `<C-d>` command to reveal a list of possible completions:

```
:Emodel <C-d>
author   comment post
```

You can then use the `<Tab>` key to cycle through the available options.

When to Use Navigation Commands

Navigation commands allow you to open files by thinking about their naming semantics, rather than thinking about their location. This is especially valuable when a codebase contains a lot of files with similar names that fall into different categories. Whenever these navigation commands are available, they are my preferred method for navigating a codebase.

The downside is that you do have to spend some time configuring these commands. If you're working on a large codebase with a lot of different types of files, then it could take a while to build up your .projections.json configuration. You don't have to define navigation commands for every type of file in your project. My advice is to add navigation commands as and when you need them. That way, you'll start by adding navigation commands for the files you access most frequently.

Tip 9

Jumping to an Alternate File

When you're test-driving code, it's helpful to be able to quickly switch between the implementation file and its corresponding unit test. Imagine a sheet of card that has the implementation code printed on one side, and the unit test printed on the other side. Switching between the model and its unit test would be as simple as turning over the card. Your text editor should make it as easy as that to switch between related files. That's where the Projectionist plugin comes to the rescue, with its :A (for alternate) command.

Preparation

This tip builds upon the material in the previous tip on page 30. If you haven't already done so, I recommend that you go back and read that tip before this one. You'll also find instructions on how to install Tim Pope's Projectionist plugin, which you'll be using again here.

Exploring the Demo Projects

For the demonstration in this tip, you'll be using two sample projects representing a skeleton blogging application. These are similar to the sample projects from the previous tip, except that they also include unit test files.

The blog-classic-tdd application places implementation files below the app subdirectory, with unit tests below the tests/unit directory:

```
blog-classic-tdd/
├── app
│   └── models
│       ├── author.js
│       ├── comment.js
│       └── post.js
└── tests
    └── unit
        └── models
            ├── author-test.js
            ├── comment-test.js
            └── post-test.js
```

The blog-modular-tdd application takes a different approach. The implementation and unit test files are siblings in the file tree:

```
blog-modular-tdd/
└── src
    └── data
        └── models
            ├── author
            │   ├── model-test.js
            │   └── model.js
            ├── comment
            │   ├── model-test.js
            │   └── model.js
            └── post
                ├── model-test.js
                └── model.js
```

Both of these applications are laid out logically according to their own conventions. In the blog-classic-tdd project, the model and unit test files are far apart on the tree structure, but the relationship between these files follows a pattern. In the blog-modular-tdd project, the relationship between model and unit test files also follows a pattern, which happens to place the files right next to each other.

Defining Alternate Files

The Projectionist plugin lets you create a link between two related files. Once you specify the relationship between one file and its alternate, Projectionist lets you follow that link by running the :A command.

Each of the sample applications contains a hidden .projections.json file in the project's root directory. Open both of these files in Vim using the -O flag so that each file opens in its own window:

```
$ cd code
$ vim -O blog-{classic,modular}-tdd/.projections.json
```

You can switch between the windows using <C-w>w.

Here's an excerpt from the blog-classic-tdd/.projections.json file:

```
{
  "app/models/*.js": {
    "type": "model",
    "alternate": "tests/unit/models/{}-test.js"
  },
  "tests/unit/models/*-test.js": {
    "type": "modelTest",
    "alternate": "app/models/{}.js"
  },
}
```

There's a lot going on here. Let's start by focusing on the alternate property for the model type. It specifies the pattern: tests/unit/models/{}-test.js. The {} will be replaced by the portion of the glob matched by the * wildcard.

For example, if you're working on the app/models/author.js file, then the word author is matched by the * in the app/models/*.js glob. Replacing {} from the alternate property with author produces the path tests/unit/models/author-test.js, which gives you the correct location for the unit test.

The modelTest declaration specifies the same relationship in the opposite direction.

This excerpt from the blog-modular-tdd/.projections.json file defines the equivalent properties for that project:

```
{
  "src/data/models/*/model.js": {
    "type": "model",
    "alternate": "src/data/models/{}/model-test.js"
  },
  "src/data/models/*/model-test.js": {
    "type": "modelTest",
    "alternate": "src/data/models/{}/model.js"
  },
}
```

Try opening the AuthorModel file, then switching to its unit test:

⇒ `:Emodel author`
⇒ `:A`

Now try opening the unit test for the CommentModel, then switch to the implementation file:

⇒ `:EmodelTest comment`
⇒ `:A`

You can use the :A and navigation commands in the blog-classic-tdd and blog-modular-tdd projects. The commands work in context, using the configuration from the closest .projections.json file.

When showing the files contained in these two sample projects, I simplified the listings by only showing model files and their tests. If you explore the book's source code yourself, you'll see that there are also adapter and serializer files in both projects. The .projections.json files also define alternates and navigation commands for these types of files, so you can experiment with running :A in any of those files.

Other Uses for Alternate Files

In this tip, I used the example of setting up a relationship between a model file and its unit test. This is just one possible case for using the :A command. You could just as well configure the alternate property to establish a relationship between a source file and its header, or a component file and its template.

The file system lets you organize your code in a hierarchical tree structure. Even in a well-organized codebase, where every file has its place, files that are closely related can end up becoming far apart on that tree structure. By defining the alternate property, you can create shortcuts between related leaf nodes. This can greatly simplify the process of switching between related files.

CHAPTER 4

Working with the Quickfix List

The material in this chapter assumes you are familiar with Vim's quickfix feature. If you need to do some background reading on it, I recommend you review Chapter 17 of *Practical Vim [Nei15]*, "Compile Code and Navigate Errors With the Quickfix List." However, the opening tip in this chapter covers some of the same ground and serves as a good refresher. The subsequent tips build on top of that material and go into more detail.

Tip 10

Running a Build and Navigating Failures

When you run a build tool and everything works fine, you can usually disregard any output the tool produced. But when the build tool fails, it may emit output that contains clues about the line of code where the failure occurred. Using Vim's compiler plugins and the :make command, you can run a build tool and capture the output so that you can refer to it later.

Better still, Vim can parse any references to filenames and line numbers, allowing you to quickly jump to the line of code where an error originated. However, the fact that Vim's built-in :make command runs synchronously can be irritating, especially for long-running builds. The Dispatch plugin solves this by providing various adapters that allow you to run build tools asynchronously.

Preparation

To follow the examples in this tip, you'll need to install Tim Pope's Dispatch plugin.[1] You can install it to your bundle package like this:

---

1.   https://github.com/tpope/vim-dispatch

```
$ cd $VIMCONFIG/pack/bundle/start
$ git clone https://github.com/tpope/vim-dispatch.git
```

Dispatch was ahead of its time when it was released in 2013. Vim had no support for running external commands asynchronously, and Neovim didn't even exist. Make sure you check out the *Introducing dispatch.vim* screencast,[2] and enjoy the unusual fanfare that announced the plugin's release.

The Dispatch plugin supports several different adapters, allowing you to pick a strategy for running async commands that suits you. For Vim 8, I recommend using the tmux adapter. For Neovim, I recommend the neovim adapter.

Enabling the tmux Adapter

The Dispatch plugin has a built-in tmux adapter, which runs programs in a tmux pane or window. To use this adapter, start a tmux session and then launch Vim inside of that session:

```
$ tmux
$ vim
```

When you run Vim inside of a tmux session, Dispatch will select the tmux adapter by default. I recommend reading *tmux 2 [Hog16]* to learn more about tmux.

Enabling the Neovim Adapter

For Neovim, you'll want to install an extra plugin: vim-dispatch-neovim[3] by Richard Adenling. This adds a neovim adapter, which makes Dispatch run programs using Neovim's terminal emulator. You can install it to your bundle package like this:

```
$ cd $VIMCONFIG/pack/bundle/start
$ git clone https://github.com/radenling/vim-dispatch-neovim.git
```

When using Neovim, Dispatch will select the neovim adapter automatically (even if you're running Neovim inside of a tmux session). This is my preferred way of using Dispatch. I find it satisfying being able to run programs asynchronously without relying on tools such as tmux. I recommend reading Chapter 5, *Neovim's Built-In Terminal Emulator*, on page 69 to learn more about Neovim's terminal emulator.

---

2.   https://vimeo.com/63116209
3.   https://github.com/radenling/vim-dispatch-neovim

Vim 8 Job Adapter for the Dispatch Plugin

If you'd like to use Vim 8's job control feature for running tasks asynchronously, you might want to try out an experimental branch of Dispatch. Instead of installing the master branch, you could install the job branch like this:

```
$ cd $VIMCONFIG/pack/bundle/start
$ git clone -b job https://github.com/tpope/vim-dispatch.git
```

The job strategy has the benefit of being self-contained, meaning that you can use Dispatch to perform async tasks without having to depend on tmux. But this strategy also has some limitations. For example, jobs aren't well-suited for commands that read from stdin, so if you're running a command that has an interactive mode, or needs to show a password prompt, the task may fail in unexpected ways. For this reason, the job branch remains experimental. With the prospect of a built-in :terminal command coming soon (see the appendix, *Adding :terminal support*, on page 130), it may be that a terminal adapter would render these issues moot.

Setting Up the Demo Project

The source code that accompanies this book includes a good-day directory. In there you'll find a simple TypeScript project called good-day. Switch to that directory and use npm to install the TypeScript compiler and its dependencies:

```
$ cd code/good-day
$ npm install
good-day@1.0.0 /Users/drew/code/good-day
├── tslint@5.7.0
└── typescript@2.5.2
```

The TypeScript compiler binary is installed in the node_modules/.bin directory. You can execute it like this:

```
$ ./node_modules/.bin/tsc --version
Version 2.5.2
```

For this tip, it's important you are able to run the TypeScript Compiler without having to specify the full path. To make this work, modify your environment so that the ./node_modules/.bin appears at the start of your path. The npm bin command outputs the full pathname for that directory:

```
$ export PATH=$(npm bin):$PATH
$ tsc --version
Version 2.5.2
```

Now, run tsc to build the project:

```
⇒ $ tsc
```

Open the build/greeting.html file in a browser with JavaScript enabled and you should see a greeting message wishing you a good day.

Making Vim Call the Compiler (a Naive Approach)

Open the sample TypeScript file in Vim:

```
⇒ $ vim src/greeting.ts
```

You can use Vim's :!{cmd} command to invoke the TypeScript compiler on the current file:

```
⇒ :!tsc --outDir build %
```

Note that the :!{cmd} runs synchronously, meaning that you can't interact with Vim until the command finishes execution. The % symbol is a shorthand for the filepath of the active buffer (:help cmdline-special). This command generates a greeting.js file in the build directory. When everything goes smoothly, the compiler produces no output on stdout.

Now, let's see what happens when things don't go so smoothly. The good-day directory contains a break-things.diff patch file. Apply the patch by running:

```
⇒ :!patch % break-things.diff
⇒ :edit! src/greeting.ts
```

Now, try compiling the TypeScript file again:

```
⇒ :!tsc --outDir build %
‹ src/greeting.ts(9,7): error TS2322: Type '1' is not assignable...
  src/greeting.ts(23,22): error TS2345: Argument of type '"now"'...
  [Process exited 2]
```

The TypeScript compiler prints a couple of error messages. These can help you fix the issues by showing you the filename, line number, and column number where each error originated. But you've got a problem: With your next keystroke, the output from :!{cmd} is dismissed. That's inconvenient if you want to refer to those error messages.

There are two things about the :!{cmd} workflow that we could improve upon. First, it would be better if the output from the build was captured in such a way that we could easily refer to it later. Next, it would be handy if there was an option to run a build asynchronously so that you could continue to interact with Vim while the build executes. We'll tackle each of these issues one by one.

Capturing Compiler Output with :make

If you want to capture the output from an external program, you should reach for the :make command (:help :make). As the name suggests, you can use this to run a build that's configured by a Makefile. But you can also use the :make command to run other types of builds. In this demonstration, we'll continue to use the TypeScript compiler.

To use the :make command, you need to configure two options: 'makeprg' and 'errorformat'. These depend upon each other, so if you change the value of 'makeprg', it's likely that you'll also want to change the value of 'errorformat' (and vice versa). The best way to ensure that you change both options simultaneously is by loading a compiler plugin.

For the demonstration in this tip, you can use this simple compiler plugin:

```
compiler/typescript.vim
let current_compiler = "typescript"
CompilerSet makeprg=tsc\ $*\ --outDir\ build\ %
CompilerSet errorformat=%+A\ %#%f\ %#(%l\\\,%c):\ %m,%C%m
```

To install this, create an after/compiler directory in your $VIMCONFIG directory. Then copy the typescript.vim file there:

```
$ mkdir -p $VIMCONFIG/after/compiler
$ cp code/compiler/typescript.vim $VIMCONFIG/after/compiler/
```

We're using the after/compiler directory (rather than compiler) to make sure this compiler overrides any other typescript compilers you may have installed on your system. Open the src/greeting.ts file in Vim, then activate the typescript compiler by running:

```
:compiler typescript
```

That sets buffer-local 'makeprg' and 'errorformat' options to the values specified in the compiler plugin. Now you can compile your TypeScript file just by running:

```
:make
!tsc  --outDir build src/greeting.ts
```

Vim executes the command specified by the 'makeprg' option, then populates the quickfix list using any output produced by that command. If you're not seeing any output, use the break-things.diff patch and run :make again. To inspect the output from the build, open the quickfix window:

```
:copen
```

You can traverse the list of errors using the commands: :cfirst, :cprev, :cnext, :clast. These commands allow you to quickly jump between errors, fixing them as you go.

TypeScript Support for Vim

As I write this, Vim has no built-in support for TypeScript (although that may have changed by the time you read this). If you'd like to add TypeScript support, you can install the typescript-vim plugin[a] by Leaf Garland. With this installed, Vim will recognize the .ts extension and enable syntax highlighting for TypeScript files. It also includes a compiler plugin for TypeScript.

---

a.   https://github.com/leafgarland/typescript-vim

Running :make Asynchronously

The killer feature of the :make command is that it populates the quickfix list, allowing you to navigate easily between any error messages. But there's a downside to this command: it runs synchronously. That means you can't interact with Vim until the build completes. This is of little consequence if your build completes quickly, but for long-running builds, it can interrupt your workflow.

You can simulate a long-running build by installing the tardyscript compiler, which is provided with this book's source code. This is identical to the typescript compiler we used earlier, except it sleeps for five seconds before launching the build:

```
$ cp code/compiler/tardyscript.vim $VIMCONFIG/after/compiler/
```

Enable the tardyscript compiler and start another build:

```
:compiler tardyscript
:make
!sleep 5;tsc --outDir build src/greeting.ts
```

This build takes at least five seconds to complete. During that time you can't interact with Vim in any way. (Now for the moment we've been building up to...)

The dispatch plugin provides a :Make command (note the capital "M"), which behaves like an asynchronous version of Vim's built-in :make command. Try it out, once again using the tardyscript compiler:

```
⇒  :compiler tardyscript
⇒  :Make
```

If you're using the neovim adapter, Dispatch opens a terminal buffer in a horizontal split and runs the program there. With the tmux adapter, Dispatch creates a new tmux pane and runs the program there. If the build fails, the output is used to populate the quickfix list and the quickfix window opens automatically. If the build succeeds, the quickfix window does not open automatically.

Dispatch also provides a :Make! variation. Try it out and observe the differences:

```
⇒  :Make!
```

With the neovim adapter, Dispatch uses jobstart() to run the program in the background. With the tmux adapter, Dispatch creates a new tmux window and runs the program there, while keeping the current tmux window active. The quickfix window doesn't automatically open when the program exits, but you can open the quickfix window at your convenience using the :Copen command.

To summarize: the :Make command lets you run a build in the *foreground*, while the :Make! command lets you run a build in the *background*. A foreground build is appropriate for shorter tasks ("build this file"), while a background build is more suitable for long-running tasks ("build the whole project"). Whichever method you choose, you can continue to operate Vim while the build executes. It makes no difference if the build takes five seconds or five minutes.

When a build is running asynchronously, you should be cautious about saving changes to files, because this could affect the build. As a rule of thumb, it's okay to use Vim for reading code, but not wise to make changes while a build is running.

Incorporating Compiler Plugins to Your Workflow

When you get the hang of Vim's compiler plugins, you might find yourself wanting to use :make for more than just building the project. For example, the quickfix list could be useful if you want to lint all of the files in your project, or if you want to run your test suite. Check out the next tip to see how the Dispatch plugin can further streamline your workflow.

Tip 11

Switching Compilers

In the previous tip, you learned how to build a project by selecting an appropriate compiler plugin then using the :make command. In a real project, things may not be so simple. You might have several different ways of building the project, depending on whether you are targeting a development or production environment. You might have other build-like tasks, such as linting your files or running your test suite. If you want to use the :make command for various different tasks, you're going to have to switch between compiler plugins.

Preparation

This tip builds on top of the material from the previous tip. Follow the steps from the Preparation section in that tip to install the Dispatch plugin and set up the demo project. In addition, copy the tsconfig and tslint compilers:

```
$ mkdir -p $VIMCONFIG/after/compiler
$ cp code/compiler/tslint.vim $VIMCONFIG/after/compiler/
$ cp code/compiler/tsconfig.vim $VIMCONFIG/after/compiler/
```

Switching Build Tools

In this demonstration, you'll use two different build tools: tslint to check for inconsistencies in coding style, and tsc to compile the project.

Open the sample TypeScript file in Vim:

```
$ cd code/good-day
$ vim src/greeting.ts
```

You can compile the TypeScript files by enabling the tsconfig compiler then using the :make command:

```
:compiler tsconfig
:make
```

You can lint the TypeScript files by enabling the tslint compiler then running :make:

```
:compiler tslint
:make
```

Now imagine that your workflow requires you to alternate frequently between linting and building your project. Each time you want to run a different build tool, you have to run two commands: :compiler followed by :make. That may not sound like much, but the friction of having to run two commands is something you want to avoid. This is where the :Dispatch command comes in handy.

Making :Dispatch Infer the Compiler

The :Dispatch {cmd} command provides a one-step solution for setting up a compiler then executing a build tool. Try using it to run the TypeScript compiler:

⇒ `:Dispatch tsc`

You should find that the quickfix list is populated using the output from the tsc command. It's as though you had run :compiler tsconfig followed by :make. That command doesn't explicitly specify a compiler, so how does the :Dispatch command know which compiler to use?

The Dispatch plugin has a clever mechanism for automatically selecting a suitable compiler plugin. It works like this: For each compiler plugin in your runtimepath, the value of 'makeprg' is compared with your specified {cmd}. If they match, that compiler is selected. Having found a suitable compiler plugin, the dispatch plugin uses the specified 'errorformat' to parse any output.

Let's take a look at the tsconfig.vim compiler:

```
compiler/tsconfig.vim
let current_compiler = "tsconfig"
CompilerSet makeprg=tsc
CompilerSet errorformat=%+A\ %#%f\ %#(%l\\\,%c):\ %m,%C%m
```

This compiler plugin sets 'makeprg' to tsc. The dispatch plugin is able to identify this as a suitable compiler plugin to use with the :Dispatch tsc command.

That's pretty smart! Let's try another one:

⇒ `:Dispatch tslint -c tslint.json 'src/**/*.ts'`

Once again, errors are parsed and used to populate the quickfix list. Dispatch is able to choose the correct compiler because the tslint compiler sets 'makeprg' to tslint:

```
compiler/tslint.vim
let current_compiler = "tslint"
let s:cpo_save = &cpo
set cpo-=C
CompilerSet makeprg=tslint\ $*\ -t\ prose\ -c\ tslint.json\ 'src/**/*.ts'
CompilerSet errorformat=
    \%EERROR:\ %f[%l\\\,\ %c]:\ %m,
    \%WWARNING:\ %f[%l\\\,\ %c]:\ %m,
    \%E%f[%l\\\,\ %c]:\ %m
let &cpo = s:cpo_save
unlet s:cpo_save
```

I want to highlight a subtle but important feature of the :Dispatch command:
it doesn't modify the 'makeprg' and 'errorformat' settings. To see this for yourself,
enable the tsconfig compiler, then inspect the 'makeprg' and 'errorformat' settings:

⇒ `:compiler tsconfig`
⇒ `:set mp? efm?`
❮ `makeprg=tsc`
`errorformat=%+A %#%f %#(%l\,%c): %m,%C%m`

Use :Dispatch to run tslint, then inspect the compiler settings again:

⇒ `:Dispatch tslint -c tslint.json 'src/**/*.ts'`
⇒ `:set mp? efm?`
❮ `makeprg=tsc`
`errorformat=%+A %#%f %#(%l\,%c): %m,%C%m`

Remember that when you run :Dispatch tslint, the output is parsed using the
'errorformat' specified by the tslint compiler. Even so, the 'makeprg' and 'errorformat'
are not altered by the :Dispatch command. That means you can continue to use
:make to build the project, while using :Dispatch to run alternative build tools.

Helping Dispatch Choose a Compiler

The good-day project includes an npm script for linting the typescript files (see
package.json for the implementation). You can run the script via npm run:

⇒ `:Dispatch npm run lint`

That takes fewer keystrokes than typing out the full tslint command with all
of its options. But there's a downside to running this script: it adds a layer
of indirection, which means that dispatch can't automatically select a suitable
compiler. In this scenario, dispatch falls back to a catch-all parser.

You can force dispatch to use a particular compiler with the -compiler flag:

⇒ `:Dispatch -compiler=tslint npm run lint`

Or, you can teach dispatch how to choose the right compiler by adding to the g:dispatch_compilers dictionary. Try putting these lines in your vimrc then reloading it:

```
let g:dispatch_compilers={}
let g:dispatch_compilers['npm run lint']='tslint'
```

This tells the dispatch plugin that when you run the npm run lint command, you want to use the tslint compiler. Try the command again:

⇒ **:Dispatch npm run lint**

This time the quickfix list is populated correctly and you can navigate the errors.

Specifying a Default :Dispatch Command

By setting the b:dispatch variable, you can specify a default {cmd} for :Dispatch. Try this:

⇒ **:let b:dispatch='npm run lint'**

Running :Dispatch is now equivalent to running :Dispatch npm run lint, with compiler selection working just as before. Setting the b:dispatch variable configures the :Dispatch command in much the same way that selecting a compiler plugin configures the :make command.

You can set things up so that :make runs your *primary* build tool, while :Dispatch runs your *secondary* build tool. In this example, tsc is the primary and tslint is the secondary.

The b:dispatch variable is scoped to the buffer, which means you can specify a different default command for each buffer. Think of the possibilities! For typescript files, tslint could be the default dispatch. For unit test files, the default could be your test runner.

You could use an autocommand to set the b:dispatch by filetype (see Tip 26, *Using Autocommands to Respond to Events*, on page 105). Better still, you could use the Projectionist plugin to set the variable for each file within a project. See Tip 28, *Setting Buffer-Local Configuration Per Project*, on page 116 for a demonstration.

Tip 12

Linting the Current File

The ALE plugin runs linting tools asynchronously on your buffer. Errors and warnings are marked with signs to make them easily visible, and you can quickly jump between them using the navigation commands provided. In this tip, you'll install the ALE plugin and eslint tool and use them to find and repair errors in a sample JavaScript file. You'll also learn how to configure ALE so that it runs your preferred linting tools for each specified filetype. And you'll learn of various ways to configure ALE so that it runs linters when manually invoked, or automatically in response to various events.

Preparation

To follow the examples in this tip, you'll need to install Andrew Wray's ALE plugin.[4] ALE stands for *asynchronous linting engine*. You can install it into your bundle package like this:

```
$ cd $VIMCONFIG/pack/bundle/start
$ git clone https://github.com/w0rp/ale.git
```

Run :helptags ALL, then you can find extensive documentation for the plugin by looking up :help ale. Next, add the following lines to your vimrc file:

ale-config/basics.vim
```
" For JavaScript files, use `eslint` (and only eslint)
let g:ale_linters = {
\   'javascript': ['eslint'],
\ }

" Mappings in the style of unimpaired-next
nmap <silent> [W <Plug>(ale_first)
nmap <silent> [w <Plug>(ale_previous)
nmap <silent> ]w <Plug>(ale_next)
nmap <silent> ]W <Plug>(ale_last)
```

Setting the g:ale_linters variable this way means that when you open JavaScript files, ALE will perform linting with the eslint tool.

You'll need the ale_first, ale_previous, ale_next, and ale_last mappings to traverse the list of warnings produced by linting tools. I've suggested mappings in the style

---

4. https://github.com/w0rp/ale

of Tim Pope's Unimpaired plugin[5] (mnemonic: "w" is for warning), but feel free to customize these to your own taste.

Setting Up the Demo Project

The source code that accompanies this book includes a linting directory. Switch to that directory and use npm to install eslint and its dependencies:

```
$ cd code/linting
$ npm install
date-in@1.0.0 /Users/drew/modvim/code/linting
└── eslint@3.19.0
...
```

You'll be using the eslint tool to find some deliberate mistakes in the sample code.

Running eslint from the Command Line

The date-in.js file looks like this:

linting/date-in.js
```
Line 1  exports.dateIn = (count=0, unit='days') => {
          const now = new Date();
          const dayInMs = 1000 * 60 * 60 * 24;
          const offset = 0;
   5
          if (/^days?$/.test(unit)) {
            offset = count * dayInMs;
          } else if (/^weeks?$/.test(unit)) {
            offset = count * dayInMs * 7;
  10      }

          const targetDate = new Date(now.getTime() + offset);
          return targetDate.toISOString().slice(0, 10)
        };
```

It contains a couple of deliberate mistakes. To identify them, run eslint on the date-in.js file like this:

```
$ ./node_modules/.bin/eslint date-in.js

/Users/drew/modvim/code/linting/date-in.js
  1:33   error  Strings must use doublequote  quotes
  7:5    error  'offset' is constant          no-const-assign
  9:5    error  'offset' is constant          no-const-assign
  13:47  error  Missing semicolon             semi

✖ 4 problems (4 errors, 0 warnings)
```

---

5.   https://github.com/tpope/vim-unimpaired

(Take a look at .eslintrc.json if you want to see how the eslint rules have been configured.)

eslint raised four problems. Each is listed with a line number, a column number, a message, and an identifier for the rule that was violated. For example, on line 1 at column 33, the quotes rule raised the error "Strings must use doublequote."

To fix these, you could navigate to them one by one using Vim's regular navigation commands. For example, 1G followed by 33| would move your cursor to the address of the first error. But it would be more convenient if Vim would parse the list and use it to generate a list of locations for you to jump between. In the next part of this tip, we'll see how to do this.

Meet the Asynchronous Linting Engine

Open the date-in.js file in Vim:

⇒ `$ cd code/linting`
⇒ `$ vim date-in.js`

If you've correctly installed ALE and eslint, you should see something like the following screenshot:

```
>>exports.dateIn = (count=0, unit=days') => {
     const now = new Date();
     const dayInMs = 1000 * 60 * 60 * 24;
     const offset = 0;

     if (/^days?$/.test(unit)) {
>>      offset = count * dayInMs;
     } else if (/^weeks?$/.test(unit)) {
>>      offset = count * dayInMs * 7;
     }

     const targetDate = new Date(now.getTime() + offset);
>>   return targetDate.toISOString().slice(0, 10)_
   };
   ~
date-in.js                              1,33            All
Strings must use doublequote. [Error/quotes]
```

At the left of the screen you can see Vim's *sign column* (also known as the "gutter"), where a symbol draws attention to each line containing a warning. The characters where a warning occurs are underlined, although this styling may appear different for you depending on your chosen color scheme.

You can quickly jump forward and back between warnings using the]w and [w mappings that you set up earlier. Note that as your cursor visits each warning, the error message is printed at the bottom of the screen. For example: jump to the first warning by pressing [W, then you'll see the message "Strings must use doublequote."

Now, go ahead and fix each of those warnings. Use whatever method feels most comfortable for you, but if you get stuck, try running these commands:

```
⇒  :1s/'/"/g
⇒  :4s/const/let
⇒  :13normal A;
```

Every time you change the buffer, ALE automatically re-runs eslint. You should see the warning markers disappearing moments after you fix each issue. Note that you don't even have to save the buffer for ALE to perform linting.

Using the Location List

The quickfix list and location list provide similar functionality, but they differ in their scope. The quickfix list is comparable to a g: variable: it's set globally (:help quickfix). By contrast, the location list is comparable to a w: variable: it's local to the current window (:help location-list). That makes the location list ideal for linting individual files: if you open two different files side by side in splits, each window will have its own location list containing errors for the buffer it contains.

By default, the ALE plugin populates the location list, rather than the quickfix list. That means you can use the :lfirst, :lprevious, :lnext, and :llast to traverse the warnings generated by linters. If you already have muscle memory for using these built-in commands you'll find them appealing, but don't overlook the ale_previous and ale_next traversal commands provided by ALE. Unlike the location list equivalents, these take your cursor position into account. I find the resulting behavior to be more intuitive.

Specifying Which Linters to Run

Out of the box, ALE supports linting tools for many different programming languages. For some languages, ALE supports multiple linters out of the box. To find out which tools are supported for the current filetype, run the following:

```
⇒  :ALEInfo
‹  Current Filetype: javascript
   Available Linters: ['eslint', 'flow', 'jscs', 'jshint', 'standard', 'xo']
   Enabled Linters: ['eslint']
   Linter Variables:
   let g:ale_javascript_eslint_executable = 'eslint'
   let g:ale_javascript_eslint_options = ''
   let g:ale_javascript_eslint_use_global = 0
   ...
```

For JavaScript files, ALE can use any of these linting tools: eslint,[6] jscs,[7] jshint,[8] flow,[9] standard,[10] and xo.[11] If you have none of these tools installed, ALE won't perform any linting on your JavaScript files. If you have all of these tools installed, ALE will run each linter on your JavaScript file, collecting all the results together. This behavior works nicely if you have two linting tools that complement each other. But the more linters you run, the greater the chance you'll end up with the same error being reported more than once.

To specify which linters you want to run for each filetype, use the g:ale_linters variable (:help g:ale_linters). Earlier on, we set g:ale_linters.javascript to ['eslint']. This ensured that only eslint would run, even if some of the other JavaScript linters had been available on your system.

Using Local or Global npm Executables

When you use npm to install a package such as eslint, you can make the program available globally, or locally for the current project only. ALE knows that local executables are placed in ./node_modules/.bin (relative to the project root), while global exectuables go in ~/node_modules/.bin.

By default, ALE tries to use a local executable, falling back to a global executable if necessary. This is handy if you work on different projects that use different versions of eslint. You can configure ALE to always use global executables, if that's your preference. For more information, look up :help ale-integrations-local-executables.

Specifying When to Run Linters

By default, ALE automatically runs linters whenever the text in a buffer changes. You might like this behavior, or you might find it distracting. It's a matter of personal preference. ALE provides configuration options, which let you specify how often linters are run with some granularity. In this section, we'll look at a few different ways of setting up ALE.

The sign column is only visible when a buffer contains errors. If you find it distracting that the sign column appears and disappears while you're typing,

---

6.   http://eslint.org
7.   http://jscs.info
8.   http://jshint.com
9.   https://flowtype.org
10. http://standardjs.com
11. https://github.com/sindresorhus/xo

you'll want to set the g:ale_sign_column_always variable to 1. Put this in your vimrc file (the lines marked default are included for illustration purposes):

ale-config/automatic.vim
```
let g:ale_lint_on_text_changed = 'always' " default
let g:ale_lint_on_save = 1                 " default
let g:ale_lint_on_enter = 1                " default
let g:ale_lint_on_filetype_changed = 1     " default
let g:ale_sign_column_always = 1
```

If you'd prefer to have ALE run linters only when a buffer is saved, you could put this in your vimrc:

ale-config/semi-automatic.vim
```
let g:ale_lint_on_text_changed = 'never'
let g:ale_lint_on_save = 1                 " default
let g:ale_lint_on_enter = 0
let g:ale_lint_on_filetype_changed = 0
```

Alternatively, you might prefer to have ALE run linters only when you invoke it by hand. If so, you can disable all autocommands. For convenience, you might also want to create a mapping to trigger the :ALELint command:

ale-config/manual.vim
```
nnoremap <Leader>l :ALELint<CR>
let g:ale_lint_on_text_changed = 'never'
let g:ale_lint_on_save = 0
let g:ale_lint_on_enter = 0
let g:ale_lint_on_filetype_changed = 0
```

One thing is common with all of these configurations: ALE always runs linters asynchronously. Whichever method you choose, you'll always be able to continue operating Vim while ALE is running linters.

Alternatives to ALE

Besides ALE, other linting plugins are available for Vim. Syntastic[12] is the most mature linting plugin, and it supports more linting tools and programming languages than any of the others. At present, Syntastic doesn't make use of the job control functionality, so Vim is blocked while linting.

Neomake[13] is another linting plugin that runs asynchronously. As well as running linters on an individual file, Neomake supports running commands that operate on an entire project.

---

12. https://github.com/vim-syntastic/syntastic
13. https://github.com/neomake/neomake

I encourage you to evaluate these plugins and weigh up the pros and cons for yourself. By their nature, these plugins don't play well together, so you'll have to pick one of them and uninstall the others.

Tip 13

Searching Files with Grep-Alikes

Grep searches the contents of files for a specified pattern. Vim's built-in :grep command executes grep and then parses the results and loads them into the quickfix list for easy navigation. While the built-in :grep command runs synchronously, the Grepper plugin makes it possible to run grep asynchronously. This means you can continue to operate Vim while the process runs in the background.

Preparation

In this tip, you'll use the Grepper plugin[14] by Marco Hinz. You can install it to your bundle package like this:

```
$ cd $VIMCONFIG/pack/bundle/start
$ git clone https://github.com/mhinz/vim-grepper.git
```

Run :helptags ALL, then you can find extensive documentation for the plugin by looking up :help grepper.

To configure the Grepper plugin for this tip, add the following lines to your vimrc file:

```
grepper-config/basic.vim
let g:grepper       = {}
let g:grepper.tools = ['grep', 'git', 'rg']

" Search for the current word
nnoremap <Leader>* :Grepper -cword -noprompt<CR>

" Search for the current selection
nmap gs <plug>(GrepperOperator)
xmap gs <plug>(GrepperOperator)
```

You'll need the <Leader>* and gs mappings later in this tip.

---

14. https://github.com/mhinz/vim-grepper

You'll also use these tools: grep, git-grep,[15] and Ripgrep.[16] It's not vital that you have all of these installed, but I'd recommend having at least two of these tools available on your system.

Using grep

Your system should have grep installed already. In the code/grepping directory, try running this command to search for the word "Waldo" in the goldrush.txt file:

```
$ cd code/grepping
$ grep -RIn Waldo goldrush.txt
goldrush.txt:6:Waldo is studying his clipboard.
goldrush.txt:10:The penny farthing is 10 paces ahead of Waldo.
```

For each match, grep outputs a filename, line number, and that line's contents.

Setting Up git-grep

You should have git installed already (if not, see *Other Software Requirements,* on page xi). To use the git-grep command, you'll have to turn the grepping directory into a Git repository:

```
$ cd code/grepping
$ git init
$ git add .
$ git commit -m "Initialize"
```

Now, try out the git-grep command:

```
$ git grep -nI Waldo goldrush.txt
goldrush.txt:6:Waldo is studying his clipboard.
goldrush.txt:10:The penny farthing is 10 paces ahead of Waldo.
```

The output from this command is identical to the output from grep.

Setting Up Ripgrep

Ripgrep is a grep-alike program that's implemented in Rust. Check out the repository's README for installation instructions.[17]

You can run Ripgrep as follows:

```
$ rg -H --no-heading --vimgrep Waldo goldrush.txt
goldrush.txt:6:1:Waldo is studying his clipboard.
goldrush.txt:10:41:The penny farthing is 10 paces ahead of Waldo.
```

---

15. https://git-scm.com/docs/git-grep
16. https://github.com/BurntSushi/ripgrep
17. https://github.com/BurntSushi/ripgrep#installation

Ripgrep's output includes the column number for each match, in addition to the usual filename, line number, and line contents.

Populating the Quickfix List with Grep Results

Change to the grepping directory, then launch Vim:

```
$ cd code/grepping
$ vim *.txt
```

You can run a grep search from inside of Vim using the built-in :grep command:

```
:grep -RIn Waldo .
./department-store.txt:1:Waldo is beside the boot counter.
./department-store.txt:7:EvilWaldo (in black/yellow) is beside the glove counter.
./goldrush.txt:6:Waldo is studying his clipboard.
./goldrush.txt:10:The penny farthing is 10 paces ahead of Waldo.
```

You'll see the same output as you did when you ran grep in the shell, but this time Vim parses the results and uses them to populate the quickfix list. Now you are able to navigate through the quickfix list using the :cnext, :cprev, :cfirst, and :clast commands.

The built-in :grep command runs synchronously, meaning you can't operate Vim until the program exits. The Grepper plugin provides an asynchronous variation of the command:

```
:GrepperGrep Waldo
```

This uses Vim's job control functionality to run grep in the background. When the job completes, the output is used to populate the quickfix list, just like when you used Vim's built-in :grep command.

Using Grepper as a Common Interface to Multiple Grep-Alikes

By setting the 'grepprg' and 'grepformat' options, you can make the built-in :grep command call other tools besides grep. Much in the same way that setting the 'makeprg' and 'errorformat' options can change the behavior of the :make command (see *Switching Build Tools*, on page 46). For example, if you want to make :grep call Ripgrep, you could apply these settings:

```
:set grepprg=rg\ -H\ --no-heading\ --vimgrep
:set grepformat=$f:$l:%c:%m
```

Suppose you want to alternate between two or more grep-alike tools. Having to set both of these options every time you switch tools is going to slow you

> ### Define an Abbreviation to Expand :grep to :GrepperGrep
>
> You can make it easier to enter long Ex commands by defining an abbreviation:
>
> ```
> cabbrev grep GrepperGrep
> ```
>
> In Command-Line mode, when you type grep followed by <Space>, it will be expanded to GrepperGrep. However, this expansion will occur *anywhere* on the command line, including at the search prompt, or in the middle of a :substitute command. We only want to perform the expansion if the prompt is : (for an Ex command) and the word grep appears at the start of the command line. This utility function makes it easy to set up an abbreviation that only expands under those conditions:
>
> grepper-config/alias.vim
> ```
> function! SetupCommandAlias(input, output)
>   exec 'cabbrev <expr> '.a:input
>       \ .' ((getcmdtype() is# ":" && getcmdline() is# "'.a:input.'")'
>       \ .'? ("'.a:output.'") : ("'.a:input.'"))'
> endfunction
> call SetupCommandAlias("grep", "GrepperGrep")
> ```
>
> If you really want to run the :grep command, use <C-v><Space> to prevent the expansion.

down. The Grepper plugin offers a couple of neat solutions to make it easy to switch between different grep-alike tools.

Using Grepper Convenience Commands

As you've seen, the :GrepperGrep command lets you call grep asynchronously and uses the results to populate the quickfix list. Grepper provides similar convenience commands for each tool that you enable. In our case, because we've enabled grep, git, and rg, we can use any of these convenience commands:

⇒ `:GrepperGrep Waldo`
⇒ `:GrepperGit Waldo`
⇒ `:GrepperRg Waldo`

Instead of using the global settings for 'grepprg' and 'grepformat', Grepper uses a dictionary of settings stored on the g:grepper variable. You can inspect the settings for Ripgrep by running:

⇒ `:echo g:grepper.rg.grepprg`
❮ `rg -H --no-heading --vimgrep`
⇒ `:echo g:grepper.rg.grepformat`
❮ `$f:$l:%c:%m`

Change rg to {tool} to inspect the settings for other tools.

This mechanism allows you to configure multiple different grep-alike tools. Switching from one tool to another just means invoking a different :Grepper{Tool} command.

Using the Grepper Prompt

If you run the :Grepper command without any arguments, you'll see a prompt where you can enter your query. Try it out, then type Waldo at the prompt and use <CR> to execute the query:

```
⇒ :Grepper
⇒ grep -RIn $* .> Waldo
❮ Found 4 matches
```

The prompt shows the command that will be executed when you press <CR>. $* is a placeholder that will be replaced with the arguments you type at the prompt. In this case, grep -RIn Waldo . is the resulting command that is executed.

What if you wanted to run the query with a different tool? That's easy: run :Grepper and press <CR>. The prompt starts off using the first tool specified in the g:grepper.tools list, which in this case is grep. Type "Waldo" at the prompt, then use the <Tab> key to cycle through the tools.

```
⇒ :Grepper
⇒ grep -RIn $* .> Waldo
⇒ git grep -nI> Waldo
⇒ rg -H --no-heading --vimgrep> Waldo
```

The prompt changes to show the command that will be run when you press <CR>. If you decide not to run the command, dismiss the prompt by pressing <Esc>.

You can streamline this workflow by creating a mapping that takes you directly to the prompt with your preferred tool. For example, you could put these mappings in your vimrc file:

```
grepper-config/prompt-mappings.vim
" Open Grepper-prompt for a particular grep-alike tool
nnoremap <Leader>g :Grepper -tool git<CR>
nnoremap <Leader>G :Grepper -tool rg<CR>
```

Now, you can press <Leader>g and start typing your query right away. Your search is executed using git-grep. If you press <Leader>G instead, the command is executed using rg. If you change your mind about which tool you want to use, press <Tab> to cycle through the list of supported tools.

Searching for the Current Word

Suppose you want to find all occurrences of a word under your cursor. To do this, use the -cword option.

To try this out, open the department-store.txt file and press gg to put your cursor at the start of the first line. The word "Waldo" should be underneath your cursor. Run :Grepper and give it the -cword option. When you press <CR>, the prompt is prefilled:

```
:Grepper -cword
grep -RIn $* .> '\bWaldo\b'
Found 3 matches.
```

Note that the current word has been wrapped with \b items. In grep, this item can be used to delimit the boundaries of a word. As a result, the search will match "Waldo" but not "EvilWaldo."

In the Preparation section for this tip, you created a mapping to trigger a search for the current word. To use it, press <Leader>*. This will execute search for the word under the cursor, using the first tool specified in the g:grepper.tools list.

Searching for the Current Selection

The Grepper plugin includes an operator that allows you to easily search for the text currently selected. The operator is not mapped to any keys by default, so you have to create a mapping before you can use it. In the Preparation section for this tip, you mapped this operator to the gs keys.

Let's try it out.

Open the department-store.txt file. Press G to go to the last line, then use gsf) to do a grep search for the text, "EvilWaldo (in black/yellow)". (Alternatively, you could use vf) to make a visual selection, then use gs to search for the selected text.) That should prefill your prompt with a query. If you press <Tab>, Grepper will cycle through the enabled tools.

```
grep -RIn $* .> -- 'EvilWaldo (in black/yellow)'
git grep -nI> -- 'EvilWaldo (in black/yellow)'
rg -H --no-heading --vimgrep> -- 'EvilWaldo \(in black/yellow\)'
```

Note that the query is not the same for all tools: the parentheses have been escaped for the rg query, but not for the grep and git-grep queries. The rg tool is able to use Rust regular expressions in a query, where the parentheses characters have special meaning. Whereas the grep and git-grep tools match parentheses literally. Grepper is smart enough to escape these special characters when necessary.

If you're curious about how this works, try inspecting the g:grepper.{tool}.escape for various tools:

```
:echo g:grepper.grep.escape
\^$.*[]
:echo g:grepper.rg.escape
\^$.*+?()[]{}|
```

As you can see here, only a few characters have special meaning in git-grep, whereas more characters need to be escaped in rg to match literally.

Adding Tool Support

One of the neat things about Grepper is that it's designed to be extended. It supports many grep-alike tools out of the box, but you can add support for new tools just by adding the necessary keys to the g:grepper dictionary.

Suppose a new grep-alike tool called Quantum Haystack comes out, which is so fast that it returns results even before you've executed your query. To add support for the qh executable, you would define the grepprg and add 'qh' to the list of supported tools:

```
let g:grepper.qh={ 'grepprg': 'qh --readmind' },
let g:grepper.tools=['qh', 'git']
```

This way you can configure your local copy of Grepper to work with the new tool. You might also consider submitting a patch to Grepper itself, adding built-in support for this new tool so that other people can use it too.

Before Grepper came out, it was common to see a Vim plugin for each grep-alike tool. For example, if you wanted to use ack, you would install the ack.vim plugin.[18] If you wanted to use ag, you would install the ag.vim plugin.[19] If you wanted to use rg, you would install the vim-ripgrep plugin.[20]

Grepper makes these single-use plugins obsolete. If you have a favorite grep-alike tool that you always want to use, you can configure Grepper to only use that tool. If you like to use different grep-alike tools depending on the circumstances, you can configure Grepper to support each of your preferred tools.

---

18. https://github.com/mileszs/ack.vim
19. https://github.com/rking/ag.vim
20. https://github.com/jremmen/vim-ripgrep

Tip 14

Running Tests and Browsing Failures

When doing test-driven development, you may need to run your whole test suite, the tests defined in one particular file, or even just a single isolated test. It would be handy if your text editor provided commands for executing tests at each of these levels of granularity. Also, wouldn't it be cool if you could leverage Vim's quickfix list so that when a test fails you could jump directly to the line of code where the error originated? In this tip, you'll learn about a plugin that handles all of this and is compatible with many different programming languages and testing frameworks.

Preparation

In this tip, you'll be using the vim-test plugin[21] by Janko Marohnić. (The plugin with the awesome strapline: "Run your tests at the speed of thought.") You can install it to your bundle package like this:

```
$ cd $VIMCONFIG/pack/bundle/start
$ git clone https://github.com/janko-m/vim-test.git
```

To demonstrate how this plugin works, I've prepared two separate demo projects. One is written in JavaScript, the other in Ruby. The following sections help you install the dependencies for each project.

Setting Up the testing-jasmine Project

Change to the testing-jasmine directory and use npm to install the dependencies:

```
$ cd code/testing-jasmine
$ npm install
```

In this project, the tests are written using the Jasmine library.[22] You can run the test suite as follows:

```
$ node_modules/.bin/jasmine
2 specs, 0 failures
Finished in 0.009 seconds
```

21. https://github.com/janko-m/vim-test
22. https://jasmine.github.io

Setting Up the testing-rb Project

Change to the directory and use Bundler to install the dependencies:

```
$ cd code/testing-rb
$ bundle install --path vendor/bundle
```

In this project, the tests are written using the RSpec library.[23] You can run the test suite as follows:

```
$ bundle exec rspec
Finished in 0.00371 seconds
2 examples, 0 failures
```

Opening Both Projects in Separate Tab Pages

We're going to open both projects in a single instance of Vim, using one tab page for each project:

```
$ cd code
$ vim -p testing-*/spec/homophone*
```

Because you were in the code directory when you started Vim, that's the working directory for each tab page. For the vim-test plugin to work properly, it expects your working directory to be the root of the project. Use the :lcd command to change the working directory for the testing-jasmine project:

```
:tabfirst
:pwd
code/
:lcd testing-jasmine
:pwd
code/testing-jasmine
```

Repeat this step for the testing-rb project:

```
:tablast
:pwd
code/
:lcd testing-rb
:pwd
code/testing-rb
```

Throughout this tip, I'll suggest that you switch to a particular project where you'll run a command and observe the results. You can use the :tabnext command (or gt) to switch between the two projects.

---

23. http://rspec.info

Test-Runner Commands

The vim-test plugin provides commands that let you run your entire test suite, a single test file, or even a single test. Let's try these out one by one.

Running the Whole Test Suite

Switch to the testing-jasmine tab and run the command:

⇒ `:tabfirst`
⇒ `:TestSuite`
❮ `node_modules/.bin/jasmine`
   `...`

This runs the jasmine executable, which executes all of the tests written using Jasmine. Now, switch to the testing-rb tab and run the same command:

⇒ `:tablast`
⇒ `:TestSuite`
❮ `bundle exec rspec`
   `...`

This time it runs the rspec command, which executes the RSpec test suite.

The :TestSuite command works so smoothly that it seems unremarkable, but there's a lot going on behind the scenes to make it work. By examining the filepath of the current buffer, as well as other clues from your environment, vim-test is able to detect which testing framework you're using. Then it finds a suitable executable to launch the test runner. The best bit is that all of this works with zero configuration.

Running the Current Test File

We've seen that vim-test makes it easy to run the entire test suite, but what if you want to just run the tests in a single file? You can do that with the :TestFile command. Switch to the testing-jasmine tab and try out the :TestFile command:

⇒ `:tabfirst`
⇒ `:TestFile`
❮ `node_modules/.bin/jasmine spec/homophonerSpec.js`
   `...`

This time the jasmine executable is given the path of the current file. Now switch to the testing-rb tab and run the same command:

⇒ `:tablast`
⇒ `:TestFile`
❮ `bundle exec rspec spec/homophoner_spec.rb`
   `...`

Once again, the rspec command is given the path of the current file.

:TestFile uses the same heuristics as the :TestSuite command to determine which test-runner command to use. In addition, it provides the necessary arguments to the test runner to make it run the tests from a single file only.

Running a Single Test

Sometimes you want to focus your test runner on one single test. That's where the :TestNearest command comes in. This finds the test closest to your current cursor position, then executes the test runner giving it the appropriate arguments to focus only on the selected test.

To try this out: Switch to the testing-jasmine tab and use G to move your cursor to the end of the file, then use the :TestNearest command:

```
⇒  :tabfirst
⇒  :normal G
⇒  :TestNearest
‹  node_modules/.bin/jasmine spec/homophonerSpec.js \
   --filter='Homophoner dictionary contains all words'
   ...
```

Repeat that process in the testing-rb project:

```
⇒  :tablast
⇒  :normal G
⇒  :TestNearest
‹  bundle exec rspec spec/homophoner_spec.rb:25
   ...
```

RSpec lets you run a single test by specifying the filename and line number where that test is defined. Jasmine doesn't have the option of providing a line number, but you can single out one test using the --filter flag. The vim-test plugin knows how to prepare the arguments for each test runner so that the nearest test is executed in isolation. How cool is that?

Re-Running the Most Recent Test Runner

When practicing test-driven development, you'll switch frequently between the test and implementation files. What if you want to use a test runner command when you don't have a test file open? That's where the :TestLast command comes in. You can use this to re-run the test runner that you used most recently.

To try this out, activate the testing-rb project and run the last test by itself:

```
⇒  :tablast
⇒  :normal G
⇒  :TestNearest
❮  bundle exec rspec spec/homophoner_spec.rb:25
   ...
```

The testing-rb directory contains a break-things.diff patch file, which will cause the tests to fail. Apply the patch, then open the implementation file:

```
⇒  :!patch lib/homophoner.rb break-things.diff
⇒  :edit! lib/homophoner.rb
```

In this context, running :TestNearest makes no sense because the active buffer is not a test file. But you can use :TestLast to re-run the last test:

```
⇒  :TestLast
❮  bundle exec rspec spec/homophoner_spec.rb:25
```

You'll see some failures this time. If you like a challenge, study the error message and see if you can fix the failing test. (Take a peek inside the break-things.diff file if you want a hint!)

Loading Test-Runner Output into the Quickfix List

vim-test supports various different *strategies* for executing test runners. By default, it uses a basic execution strategy. In Vim 8, the command is run using :!{cmd}, while in Neovim, it's run using :terminal {cmd}. Both of these methods have the same shortcoming: the output from the test runner doesn't end up in the quickfix list.

By changing the strategy you can alter how the test runner is executed. To enable the dispatch strategy, add this line to your vimrc and reload it:

```
let test#strategy = "dispatch"
```

Now, try running through each of the test-runner examples from the previous section. With the dispatch strategy activated, vim-test executes the test-runner command using :Dispatch {cmd}.

These two plugins work well together: vim-test is responsible for selecting the appropriate test-runner command, and vim-dispatch attempts to chose an appropriate compiler plugin to go with the test-runner command. For a detailed discussion of how that works, see Tip 11, *Switching Compilers*, on page 46.

As I write this, Vim ships with a compiler plugin for RSpec, but nothing for Jasmine. The RSpec compiler is part of the vim-ruby package,[24] which you

---

24. https://github.com/vim-ruby/vim-ruby

can install directly if you want to be sure you've got the latest version. You could search GitHub to see if anyone has published a Jasmine compiler plugin, or you could try writing one by yourself.

Test-Runner Support

As you saw in the earlier examples, vim-test can run tests written in RSpec and Jasmine without requiring any configuration. The plugin has built-in support for many different languages and testing tools (check out the repository's README for the full list). It's great that you can switch between projects and reuse the same test-runner commands, even when those projects use different testing frameworks. But what if you want to use a testing framework that's not supported?

You can extend vim-test to add support for any test runner. The repository's README file includes clear documentation on how to do this, and you can refer to the many built-in examples for guidance. I was able to add support for a JavaScript test runner without much difficulty.

On GitHub, you can find many examples of vim plugins that are specialized for a particular test runner or language. (The author of vim-test credits the vim-rspec[25] and vim-vroom[26] plugins as inspiration.) The vim-test plugin makes these single-purpose plugins obsolete, by providing a universal interface for running your tests.

You might find yourself wanting to customize Vim by adding test-runner commands for a particular testing framework. Rather than creating a single-purpose plugin, I'd encourage you to take the approach of extending vim-test. This way, you can benefit from the features of vim-test. And if you contribute your customizations upstream to the vim-test project, then others can benefit, too.

---

25. https://github.com/thoughtbot/vim-rspec
26. https://github.com/skalnik/vim-vroom

CHAPTER 5

Neovim's Built-In Terminal Emulator

When you run Neovim in a terminal you're never far from a shell. If you want to run a single command line, you can use :!{cmd}. Or if you want to run a series of commands, you can use <C-z> to suspend Neovim. This returns you to the shell that you used to launch the nvim process. When you're done with the shell, you can bring Neovim back into the foreground using the fg command. That brings Neovim back to life exactly as you left it.

You might be wondering: What could I do with Neovim's built-in terminal emulator that I can't already do using this suspend/resume workflow?

Use Normal Mode Commands to Interact with the Shell

When you run a shell inside of Neovim, you can interact with the shell's scrollback using Normal mode commands. That means you can scroll and search using familiar keyboard mappings. You can use text objects to select a range of text. You can yank and paste using any of Neovim's registers. You can jump to a filename under the cursor using the gf command.

This is different from enabling vi-mode keybindings in bash, or zsh, or in tmux copy mode. We're not talking about low-fidelity vi-emulation. It's what you always wanted: the real thing.

Use Neovim as a Window Manager

With the suspend/resume workflow, you can only have one thing running in the foreground at a time. You're either using Neovim, or you're using the shell.

Suppose you have a README file containing instructions on how to get up and running on a new project. You want to be able to keep that file visible so you can follow the instructions, while at the same time executing the specified commands in a shell. You need a window manager.

With Neovim, you could keep the README file open in a regular buffer, then open a split containing a shell where you do your work. You can use familiar Neovim commands to create and navigate these windows. (As a bonus, you can copy commands from the README file and paste them into the terminal buffer using standard yank/paste commands.)

Control Processes Remotely with Vim Script

When a program is running in a terminal buffer, you can interact with it programmatically using Vim script. This is really handy if you want to be able to control that process remotely from Neovim, rather than interacting with the process directly.

Suppose you're doing web development and you need to run a web server. Sometimes you need to restart the server to make it reload the latest configuration. Usually you achieve this by activating the window where the web-server process is running, stopping the server, then starting it again, before re-activating the window containing Neovim so you can continue with your work. Wouldn't it be handy if you could just run :Restart in Neovim? You'll see how to do this in Tip 19, *Sending Commands to a Terminal Buffer*, on page 85.

If you're excited by the possibilities of interacting with running processes programatically, then you're going to love using Neovim's terminal emulator.

Terminal Terminology

When discussing Neovim's terminal emulator, you might be confused by the similar sounding terms: *Terminal mode* and *terminal buffer*. Terminal mode is a mode, just like Normal mode, Insert mode, and so on (we always capitalize mode names in this book, following the convention from Vim's built-in documentation). Just as nnoremap lets you create mappings for Normal mode, tnoremap lets you create mappings for Terminal mode. You can use Terminal mode only in terminal buffers, where Insert mode is not available.

A regular Vim buffer usually corresponds to a file on disk, whereas a terminal buffer corresponds to a process. You can't directly modify the text in terminal buffer (such as using dd). Depending on what program is running within, you may be able to indirectly modify the contents of a terminal buffer by interacting with the underlying program. To interact with the program running inside a terminal buffer, you activate Terminal mode.

As a final note, Vim also has Command-Line mode, which shouldn't be confused with Terminal mode. You can activate Command-Line mode from Normal mode by pressing /, ?, or :. This mode allows you to run the search command and to run Ex commands.

Tip 15

Grokking Terminal Mode

 Neovim only

As a Vim user, you're used to hopping between modes that are specialized for particular tasks. You spend most of your time in Normal mode, where you can use motions to move around and operators to modify the text in a document. You can switch to Insert mode if you want to add text to a document. Visual mode is useful when you want to select and manipulate text. And Command-Line mode lets you run Ex commands such as :w and :q, as well as the search command.

In Neovim, you get a new mode to play with: Terminal mode. In this mode, you can interact with programs that run inside the built-in terminal emulator.

Preparation

In this tip, you'll be running a shell inside of a Neovim terminal buffer. If you use the bash shell with default readline keybindings (also known as emacs-mode), then you should be able to follow this tip seamlessly. If you use a different shell, or if you've customized the keybindings for your shell, then some of the commands may not work for you as described. In this case, you may need to translate the suggested keystrokes to something that works with your setup.

Launching a Shell

If you run the :terminal command with no arguments, Neovim opens a terminal buffer running a shell:

⇒ `:terminal`

Having just created a terminal buffer, you start out in Normal mode. Pressing the i key switches you to Terminal mode, which is indicated by the -- TERMINAL -- message at the bottom left of the screen. Pressing the `<C-\><C-n>` keys switches you back to Normal mode again. This might feel a bit awkward at first. You will soon find out how to create a mapping to exit Terminal mode more easily, but for now we will make do with the defaults. Now try switching between Terminal mode and Normal mode a few times to get used to those commands.

Insert mode is not available in terminal buffers. In regular text buffers, you use i, a, I, and A to switch from Normal mode to Insert mode. In terminal buffers, these same keystrokes switch from Normal mode to Terminal mode.

Using Terminal Mode

In Terminal mode, any keys you press will be forwarded to the underlying program (apart from <C-\><C-n>, which switches to Normal mode). Right now, the underlying program is a bash shell. Let's switch to Terminal mode and interact with the shell by running some basic commands:

```
⇒  » cd code/terminal
⇒  » pwd
‹  ~/drew/modvim/code/terminal
⇒  » ls
‹  lorem-ipsum.txt              termcursor.vim
   nvim-setup-instructions.md   terminal-mode-escape.vim
   readme.md
⇒  » cat readme.md
‹  Neovim's terminal emulator is cool.
```

In this context, Terminal mode feels similar to Insert mode in that it lets you input text at the current command line. Pressing <CR> executes the command line. If you're using the bash shell with default readline bindings (emacs-mode), then you can move the terminal cursor using mappings such as <C-a>, <C-e>, <M-b>, and <M-f>. These mappings are interpreted by the underlying program, which in this case is the shell. All that Neovim does is to forward your keystrokes to the program that's running inside the terminal emulator.

Now run the top command to launch a new process inside your shell:

```
⇒  » top
```

If you press ?, you'll see a brief page of documentation for top. If you press q you'll quit the process and return to your shell. As before, Neovim is simply forwarding your keystrokes to the underlying program, but top and bash have different ways of interpreting the q and ? keys.

When you're in Terminal mode, your interactions with the underlying program feel just like they would if that program were running in any other terminal emulator. What makes Neovim's terminal emulator special is that fact that you can also switch to Normal mode and use familiar commands to scroll the text, as well as copying and pasting using Vim's registers. We'll explore this capability in detail in Tip 18, *Using Normal Mode Commands in a Terminal Buffer*, on page 82. First, let's reduce the friction of moving between Normal mode and Terminal mode.

Switching Between Terminal Mode and Normal Mode

When I first started using Neovim's terminal buffers, I kept expecting to be able to use the `<Esc>` key to switch from Terminal mode back to Normal mode. After all, that's how you get back to Normal mode from Insert mode, from Visual mode, and from Command-Line mode.

You can use the :tnoremap command to create a mapping that applies only in Terminal mode (:help :tnoremap). Try running this:

⇒ `:tnoremap <Esc> <C-\><C-n>`

Now, you can switch from Terminal mode back to Normal mode by pressing they `<Esc>` key. That brings a bit more consistency to the experience of using terminal buffers. But you've created a new problem: you can no longer send an Escape key to the program running inside the terminal buffer.

To avoid this problem, create another mapping. Try copying these lines into your vimrc file, then save it and run :source ~/.vimrc:

```
terminal/terminal-mode-escape.vim
if has('nvim')
  tnoremap <Esc> <C-\><C-n>
  tnoremap <C-v><Esc> <Esc>
endif
```

Now you can send an Escape key to the terminal by pressing `<C-v><Esc>` (mnemonic: Verbatim escape). I suggest this mapping because it feels idiomatic: in Insert mode, you can use `<C-v>{nondigit}` to enter a nondigit character literally (:help i_ctrl-v). This allows you to insert a tab character by pressing `<C-v><Tab>`, even when the tab key has been configured to insert spaces.

Distinguishing the Terminal Cursor from the Normal Cursor

In a terminal buffer, you have not one but two cursors: the *Terminal cursor*, which is managed by the underlying program, and the *Normal cursor*, which is managed by Vim. This is easier to demonstrate than to describe, so read on for a better understanding.

Type out a short command line, but don't press <CR> just yet:

⇒ » `echo 'hello'`

While still in Terminal mode, move your cursor to the start of the command line (you can use <C-a> if your shell is configured to use emacs bindings). Take note of where your cursor is, then switch to Normal mode. You could go back into Terminal mode either by pressing i, I, a, or A. Here's a quiz: Which one would you use if you wanted to switch back to Terminal mode with your cursor placed at the end of the command line?

It's a trick question—the answer is none of them! When you switch to Terminal mode, the cursor always resumes from where it left off. i, I, a, and A all do the same thing.

To make this more obvious, try running this command:

⇒ `:highlight! TermCursorNC guibg=red guifg=white ctermbg=1 ctermfg=15`

Now switch to Terminal mode and move the cursor at the end of the line (you can use <C-e> if your shell is configured with emacs bindings). When you return to Normal mode, the location of the terminal cursor should be picked out in an obvious red.

Try out some Normal mode motions, such as b, w, 0, G, k, and j. Vim's cursor moves freely, but the terminal cursor stays put. You can only move the terminal cursor when you're in Terminal mode.

The terminal cursor should be easily visible inside and outside of Terminal mode. If the color scheme you are using doesn't style the TermCursor and TermCursorNC syntax groups (:help hl-TermCursor), I suggest adding these lines to your color scheme:

terminal/termcursor.vim
```
if has('nvim')
  highlight! link TermCursor Cursor
  highlight! TermCursorNC guibg=red guifg=white ctermbg=1 ctermfg=15
endif
```

Of course, you can tweak the colors to match the color scheme's palette.

Tip 16

Running Programs in a Terminal Buffer

 Neovim only

Neovim can run external processes and capture their output in a terminal buffer. These buffers are displayed in Vim's windows just like any other buffer. In this tip, you'll learn how to create a terminal buffer and how to kill the process running within.

Starting Programs in a Terminal Buffer

Let's start by reviewing some of the methods that Vim provides for running external programs. You can use the :!{cmd} command to execute a command in a shell. To see how this works, use cat to inspect the contents of the /etc/shells file:

```
:!cat /etc/shells
# List of acceptable shells for chpass(1).
/bin/bash
/bin/csh
/bin/ksh
/bin/sh
/bin/tcsh
/bin/zsh
/usr/local/bin/bash
Press ENTER or type command to continue
```

The output from the command is echoed beneath Neovim's command line. If you press any key, the command's output is dismissed and there's no way to restore it. The :!{cmd} command is useful in scenarios where you want to execute a command that exits quickly, and whose output is of no great interest.

If you want to capture the output from a command so that you can refer to it later, you could instead use the :read !{cmd} command. To see how this works, create a new buffer then use the same cat command as before:

```
:new
:read !cat /etc/shells
8 more lines
```

This executes the specified command and appends its output into the current buffer at the cursor location. The :read !{cmd} command is useful if you want to capture the output from a command in an existing buffer.

The :!{cmd} and :read !{cmd} commands have long been available in Vim, but the :terminal {cmd} command is a new feature in Neovim (:help :terminal). (If you don't want to type out the full word you can abbreviate the command to :te {cmd}, which is almost as brief as the "bang" command!) To see how this works, use the same cat command as before:

⇒ `:terminal cat /etc/shells`

Superficially, this appears to accomplish the same thing as when you ran :new followed by :read !{}. In both cases, the command's output is captured in a buffer. But whereas :read !{} simply appends the output into the current buffer, the :terminal command creates a special type of buffer called a *terminal buffer*. You can identify these special buffers in the buffer list by their name, which takes the form term://{cwd}//{pid}:{cmd}, where cwd stands for current working directory and pid is the process id:

⇒ `:ls`
‹
```
  1 #h + "[No Name]"                   line 12
  2 %a-  "term://.//37714:cat /etc/shells" line 13
```

You can't modify the text in a terminal buffer directly. Instead, the text is updated asynchronously by the program running inside the terminal buffer. The cat program doesn't illustrate this well because it produces all of its output at once and then exits. Try launching a long-running process in a terminal buffer using the top program:

⇒ `:terminal top`

This gives a good illustration of what's special about a terminal buffer. The top program draws a textual user interface (TUI), which takes up all of the available screen space. Every second or so, the buffer's contents are completely rewritten. If you try to modify the buffer directly, you get an error message:

⇒ `:%delete`
‹ `E21: Cannot make changes, 'modifiable' is off`

You'll see the same error when using Normal mode commands such as dd. Commands that would normally modify the text are no use in a terminal buffer, but you can use Normal mode commands to scroll the window, search for text, copy text into a buffer, and so on. See Tip 18, *Using Normal Mode Commands in a Terminal Buffer*, on page 82 for examples.

So far, we've used the :terminal command to run cat and top programs. If you run the :terminal command without the {cmd} argument, then your default shell will be started in a new terminal buffer:

```
⇒ :terminal
⇒ :ls
‹    1 %a-  "term://.//39061:/usr/local/bin/bash" line 12
```

You'll have to switch into Terminal mode if you want to interact with the shell. See Tip 15, *Grokking Terminal Mode*, on page 71 for details.

While the :!{cmd} and :read !{cmd} still have their uses, the flexibility of the :terminal {cmd} command makes it a powerful addition to your toolbox.

Hiding a Terminal Buffer

Open a new terminal buffer:

```
⇒ :terminal while true; do date; sleep 1; done
```

That one-liner creates a loop that prints the time once every second. Now let's see what happens when you hide this terminal buffer. First, make sure that only one window is visible in the current tab page, then open another buffer containing a file. Your vimrc file is always handy, so let's open that:

```
⇒ :only
⇒ :edit $MYVIMRC
```

The buffer containing your vimrc file takes over the current window, causing the terminal buffer to become hidden. In this case, the terminal buffer becomes the alternate file for the current window (:h alternate-file), which means you can cycle between those two buffers by pressing <C-^>.

Even when the terminal buffer isn't visible, the while loop continues to run in the background. If the while loop has filled the window with output, it may appear as though the process has stopped. Press G to jump to the last line of the terminal buffer. You should find timestamps are still being printed every second.

Now imagine that instead of running a while loop, you launched a web server. You could hide that buffer and the server would continue to run in the background. In Tip 19, *Sending Commands to a Terminal Buffer*, on page 85, we'll develop this idea further, by creating a command to restart the server.

Stopping Terminal Buffer Processes

Now you know how to start a process in a terminal buffer. You're going to need to know how to stop those processes as well.

Stop the Process by Interacting with It Directly

Start a fresh instance of Neovim, then run these commands:

```
:terminal while true; do date; sleep 1; done
:terminal top
:terminal
:ls
  1  h-   "term://.//40556:while true; do date; sleep 1; done" line 3
  2 #h-   "term://.//40565:top"              line 23
  3 %a-   "term://.//40575:/usr/local/bin/bash" line 9
```

One method for stopping a process is to engage with it directly and send an interrupt signal. For example, use :1b to switch to the first buffer, then activate Terminal mode by pressing i. You can stop the while loop by pressing <C-c>. The terminal buffer is still there (and you can still interact with the contents), but the process is no longer running.

Now, try using the same method to stop the other processes. The general formula is this: switch to the terminal buffer, then activate Terminal mode and send an interrupt signal. In the case of the top process, you can use either q or <C-c> as an interrupt signal. In the case of the shell, you can type the word exit then press Enter. This method for stopping a process is granular, but the details may differ depending on what process you're targeting.

Stop the Process by Deleting the Terminal Buffer

Let's look at another method that works the same way for all terminal buffers. First, set things up by starting the same three processes as before:

```
:te while true; do date; sleep 1; done
:te top
:te
:ls
  4  h-   "term://.//44932:while true; do date; sleep 1; done" line 3
  5 #h-   "term://.//44958:top"              line 23
  6 %a-   "term://.//44969:/usr/local/bin/bash" line 17
```

If you delete a terminal buffer, then the process running within that buffer will be stopped. Try using the :bwipeout! command to stop the top process:

```
:5bwipeout
E89: term://.//44958:top will be killed (add ! to override)
:5bwipeout!
:ls
  4  h-   "term://.//44932:while true; do date; sleep 1; done" line 3
  6 %a-   "term://.//44969:/usr/local/bin/bash" line 22
```

I prefer using this method, because the steps are the same regardless of which process you are targeting.

Stop All Terminal Processes by Shutting Neovim Down

When you quit Neovim, any processes running in terminal buffers will be shut down:

⇒ `:qa!`

That's the quickest way to shut everything down. Note that if you press `<C-z>` to suspend Neovim, then all processes running in terminal buffers will also be suspended. When you resume Neovim, those processes will also resume.

If you have one or more processes running in terminal buffers when you record a session, then those processes will be restarted when you load that session. Check out Tip 25, *Restarting Terminal Processes When Resuming a Session*, on page 101 for more details.

What's Next?

Have you noticed that the :terminal command opens a buffer using the current window? If you'd like to learn how to open the terminal buffer in a split (or a new tab page), read the next tip.

Tip 17

Managing Windows That Contain Terminal Buffers

 Neovim only

Neovim's splits and tab pages can display terminal buffers in just the same way that they display regular text buffers. That opens up a new possibility: you can use Neovim as a simple window manager not just for text files, but for any programs that you can run in a terminal.

Open up a simple text file in Neovim:

⇒ `$ cd code/terminal/`
⇒ `$ nvim readme.md`

Now open a new terminal buffer running your shell:

⇒ `:terminal`

Notice that the :terminal command takes over the current window, and the buffer containing readme.md is hidden. This is similar to how the :edit {file} command works.

Opening Terminal Buffers in a New Window

If you want to open a terminal buffer in a new window, you could do so by running these two commands:

⇒ `:split`
⇒ `:terminal`

Alternatively you could use this one-liner, which has exactly the same effect:

⇒ `:split | terminal`

In Ex commands, the | character behaves as a command separator (:help :bar). You could use the same technique to open a terminal buffer in a vertical split, or in a new tab page. The following table summarizes how these work.

Command	Effect
:terminal {cmd}	Terminal buffer is created in the current window
:split | terminal {cmd}	Terminal buffer is created in a horizontal split
:vsplit | terminal {cmd}	Terminal buffer is created in a vertical split
:tabedit | terminal {cmd}	Terminal buffer is created in a new tab page

If you omit the | character, the meaning of these commands is totally different. For example, :split terminal creates a text buffer called terminal, and if you :write it, you'll end up with a file on disk called terminal!

Easy Window Switching

Open your vimrc file in a fresh tab page, then open a new terminal buffer in a vertical split:

⇒ `:tabedit $MYVIMRC`
⇒ `:vsplit | terminal`

Your workspace is now divided into two windows, with a terminal buffer on the left and your vimrc file on the right. In Normal mode, you can use <C-w>h and <C-w>l to switch between the left and right windows. You can also use

<C-w>j and <C-w>k to switch down and up, if your workspace contains horizontal splits.

Press <C-w>h to activate the split window containing the terminal buffer, then switch to Terminal Mode by pressing i. In this context, how do you switch to the other window containing your vimrc file?

First, you need to switch back to Normal mode, which means pressing <C-\><C-n>, then you can use <C-w>w to switch windows. That's four keystrokes in total. Surely we can do better than that? Try putting this in your vimrc file and reloading it:

```
terminal/window-switching.vim
nnoremap <M-h> <c-w>h
nnoremap <M-j> <c-w>j
nnoremap <M-k> <c-w>k
nnoremap <M-l> <c-w>l
if has('nvim')
  tnoremap <M-h> <c-\><c-n><c-w>h
  tnoremap <M-j> <c-\><c-n><c-w>j
  tnoremap <M-k> <c-\><c-n><c-w>k
  tnoremap <M-l> <c-\><c-n><c-w>l
endif
```

The tnoremap command lets us create a mapping that applies only in Terminal mode. With these mappings defined, it doesn't matter if you're in Normal mode or Terminal mode, you can switch to another window by pressing <M-h>, <M-j>, <M-k>, or <M-l>. For the sake of completeness, you might also want to define equivalent mappings for Insert mode and Visual mode.

Seamlessly Navigating tmux Panes and Vim Windows

In Vim, you can divide your workspace using windows. In tmux, you can divide your workspace using panes. The terminology is different, but Vim windows and tmux panes are conceptually similar.

The vim-tmux-navigator plugin[a] lets you use the same mappings for navigating Vim windows and tmux panes. It's an ingenious solution, which brings to my mind the image of a Rube Goldberg machine.[b] I used to run Vim inside of tmux because I liked being able to send commands from Vim to a terminal running in a separate tmux pane. For this use case, I now prefer using Neovim's built-in terminal emulator. The fact that I can use Vim's window switching commands is an added bonus.

_____

a.   https://github.com/christoomey/vim-tmux-navigator
b.   https://en.wikipedia.org/wiki/Rube_Goldberg_machine

Tip 18

Using Normal Mode Commands in a Terminal Buffer

 Neovim only

Most Normal mode commands work in terminal buffers just as they would in regular text buffers. In this tip we'll run through some examples of the commands that are useful in this context.

Preparation

The source code that accompanies this book includes a terminal directory. Switch to that directory, then start Neovim with a terminal buffer:

```
$ cd code/terminal
$ nvim +terminal
```

This last command is equivalent to running nvim to launch Neovim, then running the :terminal Ex command after Neovim has launched (see :h +c). The examples throughout this tip should be run within this internal shell.

Copying and Pasting

Just like in regular buffers, you can copy text from a terminal buffer into any of Vim's registers. You can also paste the contents of a register into a terminal buffer, although the result depends on which program is running in the terminal buffer.

In the code/terminal directory, you'll find a nvim-setup-instructions.md file. Press i to switch to Terminal mode, then print the contents of that file using cat:

```
» cat nvim-setup-instructions.md
Run the following commands:

* `mkdir -p ~/.config/nvim`
* `touch ~/.config/nvim/init.vim`

These commands are safe if `init.vim` already exists.
```

Now switch back to Normal mode and move the cursor to the line with the mkdir instruction. Pressing yi` copies the text inside the backticks into Vim's unnamed register, then you can paste that text at the location of the terminal cursor using p. To execute that command, you have to switch to Terminal mode then press <CR>. Repeat the same steps to copy and paste the touch instruction.

The copy and paste commands work more or less as you would expect. You can prefix the yank and put commands with a named register (for example, "a), or you could use a special register such as "* to reference the system clipboard.

There's one significant difference in behavior to watch out for, though. In a text buffer, the p command inserts text next to the location of Vim's cursor; however, in a terminal buffer, the p command always inserts text at the location of the terminal cursor. This makes sense when you consider that terminal buffers are not modifiable.

Scrolling

In a terminal buffer, you can scroll up and down using familiar Normal mode commands.

In the code/terminal directory, you'll find a lorem-ipsum.txt file. If you print the contents of that file in your shell, it should fill the screen with more text than you can view all at once:

```
» clear
» cat lorem-ipsum.txt
Lorem ipsum dolor sit amet...
...
```

Quickly jump back to the top of your scrollback using the gg command. Jump to the bottom again using the G command. If there's a program running in the shell that continually outputs text, the bottom of the buffer becomes a moving target. Pressing the G key causes the buffer to automatically scroll so that the last line is always visible.

In Normal mode, the j and k commands move Vim's cursor down and up one line at a time. You might be tempted to use this to scroll the screen, but instead I recommend using the <C-e> and <C-y> commands. These scroll the buffer down and up one line at a time. The table on page 84 summarizes these and several other useful Normal mode commands for scrolling.

Use Vim's standard search commands to find patterns in the shell's scrollback. For example, suppose you need to find occurrences of the word "duo" in the shell's scrollback. You can do this by running: /duo<CR>, which moves the cursor to the next match. (Try it! The "lorem ipsum" sample contains a few matches for that pattern.) Then, use n to repeat the search or N to reverse it.

Command	Effect
gg	Jump to top of scrollback
G	Jump to bottom of scrollback
<C-y>	Scroll up one line
<C-e>	Scroll down one line
<C-u>	Scroll up half a page
<C-d>	Scroll down half a page
<C-b>	Scroll up a page
<C-f>	Scroll down a page

Jumping to a Filepath

When the cursor is positioned on a filepath, you can use the gf command to open that file in a buffer. This works in a terminal buffer just as you would expect. Let's try it out. Use the find command to output a list of filepaths:

```
» pwd
/Users/drew/modvim/code/terminal
» find $PWD
/Users/drew/modvim/code/terminal
/Users/drew/modvim/code/terminal/lorem-ipsum.txt
/Users/drew/modvim/code/terminal/nvim-setup-instructions.md
/Users/drew/modvim/code/terminal/readme.md
...
```

Switch back to Normal mode and position your cursor on one of the absolute filepaths, then use the gf command. That opens the specified file in a buffer, which takes over the current window. The terminal buffer is now hidden, but you can quickly switch back to it using the <C-^> command (:h ctrl-^).

This is really handy when running a failing build or test suite. If the output includes the filename (and line number) where the failure originated, just use gf to investigate.

Using Normal Mode Operations to Edit a Command Line in the Shell

You might be tempted to use Normal mode commands to edit the current command line. This doesn't work. Remember, the text in a terminal buffer cannot be modified by Normal mode commands. Instead, switch to Terminal mode and then invoke <C-x><C-e>, which opens the current command line in your preferred editor. See Tip 22, *Using an Existing nvim Instance as the Preferred Editor*, on page 91 for more details.

Tip 19

Sending Commands to a Terminal Buffer

 Neovim only

With Terminal mode, you can interact directly with a process running inside a terminal buffer. It's also possible to interact with such a process by remote control, by calling the jobsend() function. The beauty of this is that you can use Vim script to automate certain interactions with a program. In this tip, you'll create a simple :Restart command that you can use to restart a web server.

Preparation

The source code that accompanies this book includes a webapp directory. Switch to that directory and install the dependencies using npm:

```
$ cd code/webapp
$ npm install
```

Now open a terminal emulator in Neovim:

```
$ nvim +terminal
```

Activate Terminal mode and start running the webserver inside Neovim:

```
» npm run server
```

Open your web browser and load http://localhost:3000. You should see the words "Hello World!" Switch back to Normal mode and open the app.js file in a split:

```
:split app.js
```

Find the text that says "Hello World!" and change it to say "Hello Neovim!". In your browser, refresh the page. Nothing has changed. It still says "Hello World!" as it did before. You'll have to restart the webserver if you want to make it serve the latest version.

Back in Neovim, activate the window containing the terminal buffer, then switch to Terminal mode. Press <C-c> to stop the webserver, then restart it again by running:

```
» npm run server
```

Now switch to your browser and refresh the page. This time you should see the words "Hello Neovim!"

Restarting the server involves a lot of ceremony. Wouldn't it be cool if you could simply run a :Restart command? Since you're running the webserver inside of a Neovim terminal, this is easily done.

Sending Keys to a Terminal Buffer

You can write to the stdin of a process running in a terminal buffer using the jobsend() function (:help jobsend()). This accepts two arguments: the {job}, and the {data} to be sent.

Activate the window containing the terminal buffer that's running your webserver, then run this command:

```
:echo b:terminal_job_id
1
```

That tells us that the job ID is 1, so we can use this as the first argument when we call jobsend({job}, {data}).

To restart the webserver, run this command:

```
:call jobsend(1, "\<C-c>npm run server\<CR>")
```

You're already familiar with the <C-c> notation when defining mappings. In this context, you need to prefix that notation with a backslash to get the desired effect. When defining the second argument, make sure you use double-quotes and not single-quotes.

Running that command should have the same effect as if you had typed those keystrokes in Terminal mode. As a result, the webserver restarts.

Creating an Ad-Hoc Command to Restart the Server

It's cool that you can control a terminal buffer remotely, but you don't want to be typing out the full :call jobsend() command every time you need to restart the server. Let's create a custom command:

```
:command! Restart call jobsend(1, "\<C-c>npm run server\<CR>")
```

You can now restart the webserver just by typing:

```
:Restart
```

Now let's take this custom command for a spin. Activate the window containing the app.js file and change the response to say something else. Write the file and use your new :Restart command, then reload the page in your browser and you should see the change instantly. That allows for a much smoother workflow.

In its current form, the :Restart command is useful only for this specific editing session. There would be no point in saving this command in your vimrc file, because next time you need it the job ID of the terminal buffer could be something different. I'd call this an ad-hoc command: one to use now and throw away later. Don't be shy about creating commands like this one.

Having to restart a server is a real problem you might encounter in the real world. The solution presented in this tip is not necessarily the best solution for this problem. Another way of approaching this would be to set up a process that watches your file system and restarts the webserver automatically each time a file is updated. (Indeed, some webservers have this capability built in.) If that approach is not possible for whatever reason, then the solution presented in this tip is a good fallback.

I want this tip to inspire you. Perhaps you never thought of running a web server from inside your text editor. Does this give you ideas for other processes that you could control remotely?

Tip 20

Applying Customizations to Your Shell in a Terminal Buffer

 Neovim only

At a glance, you may not be able to tell whether a shell is running within a terminal buffer or outside of Neovim. In this tip, you'll find out how you can customize the prompt for your shell so that it appears differently inside of a terminal buffer.

Open a shell in a terminal outside of Neovim and take note of how your prompt looks. Then launch Neovim with a shell running inside a terminal buffer:

```
$ nvim +terminal
```

Can you tell which shell is running inside of Neovim and which one is running outside? You could make it more obvious by changing how the prompt looks in each context. In the bash shell, this is done by setting the $PS1 environment variable.

Detecting That a Shell Is Running Inside a Terminal Buffer

When Neovim starts up, it sets the $NVIM_LISTEN_ADDRESS environment variable. In the start up script for your shell, you can test for the presence of this variable. If $NVIM_LISTEN_ADDRESS is set, then you can assume that the shell is running inside of a terminal buffer.

Try adding this snippet to your bashrc file:

```
terminal/bash-prompt.sh
if [ -n "$NVIM_LISTEN_ADDRESS" ]; then
  export PS1="» "
else
  export PS1="\$ "
fi
```

Try starting two new shells as you did earlier: one inside a terminal buffer, the other outside. You should now be able to tell the two apart just by looking at the prompt.

You can use this technique to set up environment variables and aliases, so that your shell behaves differently inside and outside of a terminal buffer. For another example of how this can be useful, read the next tip.

Tip 21

Avoiding Nested Neovim Instances

 Neovim only

Any command that you can launch in an external shell can also be run in a terminal buffer. That includes the nvim command itself, meaning you can start a new instance of Neovim inside an existing instance. This scenario is best avoided. In this tip, you'll learn how the neovim-remote tool allows you to open files in the existing Neovim instance. You'll also see how to set up a shell alias to prevent you from accidentally creating nested instances of Neovim.

How Can Neovim Run Inside of Neovim?

Use this command to start a fresh instance of Neovim and start a terminal buffer inside:

⇒ `$ nvim +terminal`

Press i to switch to Terminal mode, then run:

⇒ `» nvim`

You are now running an instance of Neovim inside of a Neovim terminal buffer. Watch your step!

See if you can make it work: Switch to Insert mode and enter some text, then switch back to Normal mode and run :w to write the buffer. As long as you keep the outer nvim instance in Terminal mode, then all of your keystrokes will be forwarded to the inner nvim instance. When you exit Terminal mode, your keystrokes will be handled by the outer nvim instance again.

If you found that easy, try launching a terminal buffer in the inner nvim, then start another nvim instance inside that. Can you keep track of which mode each instance of Neovim is in?

It's a bad idea to run a modal text editor inside of a modal text editor. You shouldn't have to think hard to figure out what's going to happen when you type :qa!.

Using neovim-remote to Open a File in the Current Neovim Instance

Instead of opening a file in a nested Neovim instance, wouldn't it make more sense to use the existing instance of Neovim? That's where neovim-remote comes in handy. If you haven't already installed it, check out *Installing neovim-remote*, on page 9 for instructions. Note that while the tool is called neovim-remote, the executable is nvr.

Start by launching a fresh Neovim terminal emulator:

⇒ `$ nvim +terminal`

Switch to Terminal mode and run:

⇒ `» nvr ~/.config/nvim/init.vim`

That opens a buffer containing the contents of your init.vim file. By default, this command behaves like :edit, in that it opens the specified file in the current window. (Use `<C-^>` to quickly switch back to the terminal buffer.) You can specify flags to make nvr open a file in another window or tab page, as this table summarizes:

Command	Effect
nvr <file>	Open file in the current window
nvr -l <file>	Open file in the last active window
nvr -o <file> [<file> ...]	Open file(s) via :split
nvr -O <file> [<file> ...]	Open file(s) via :vsplit
nvr -p <file> [<file> ...]	Open file(s) via :tabedit

Using a Shell Alias to Prevent Accidental Nesting

Now that you know how neovim-remote works, you're going to start using it all the time, right? But first you have to train your fingers to type nvr. If you accidentally type nvim, next thing you know you'll be looking up StackOverflow to find out how to quit a nested Neovim.

You could set up a simple alias like this:

```
terminal/alias-nvim-echo.sh
if [ -n "$NVIM_LISTEN_ADDRESS" ]; then
  alias nvim='echo "No nesting!"'
fi
```

This alias will be defined only when bash is running inside a terminal buffer (see Tip 20, *Applying Customizations to Your Shell in a Terminal Buffer*, on page 87). If you use the nvim executable outside of Neovim, it will work as normal. But if you try and use the nvim command inside a terminal buffer, you'll see a message instead:

```
» nvim
No nesting!
```

This prevents you from accidentally launching a nested instance of nvim.

Alternatively, you could take this a step further and alias nvim to nvr:

```
terminal/alias-nvim-nvr.sh
if [ -n "$NVIM_LISTEN_ADDRESS" ]; then
  if [ -x "$(command -v nvr)" ]; then
    alias nvim=nvr
  else
    alias nvim='echo "No nesting!"'
  fi
fi
```

This creates the alias only if the nvr executable is available (otherwise it sets up the same echo alias as before). Having defined this alias, you can type nvim <file> inside a terminal buffer and it will actually call nvr <file>. If you chose to take this approach, bear in mind that some of the flags that you pass to the nvim command might mean something different to the nvr command.

This technique prevents you from *directly* starting a nested instance of Neovim, but it doesn't prevent you from doing so *indirectly*. For example, if you have configured Git to use Neovim as your preferred text editor, then running git commit in a terminal buffer would open a nested instance of Neovim. In the next tip, you'll find out how to avoid this scenario.

Tip 22

Using an Existing nvim Instance as the Preferred Editor

 Neovim only

Some command-line programs may invoke a text editor so that the user can compose a message. By convention, the $VISUAL environment variable is used to specify the users' preferred text editor. If you configure nvim as your prefer- ence, then it's easy to accidentally launch nested instances of Neovim. It's preferable if you can use an existing instance of Neovim, rather than starting a new one. You can set this up using neovim-remote.

Preparation

Command-line programs that require input from the user may give the option of opening a temporary file in a text editor. When you save and close that file, its contents are used by the program that invoked the editor. The $VISUAL variable is used to indicate your preferred text editor.

Open a new terminal running the bash shell, then run this command:

```
$ export VISUAL='nvim'
```

In the following sections, you'll see two examples of programs that invoke your preferred editor. I suggest that you run through each of these examples three times: the first time, use an external shell (outside of Neovim) with $VISUAL set to 'nvim'. The second time, use a shell running inside of a terminal buffer with $VISUAL set to 'nvim'. Finally, use a shell running inside of a terminal buffer with $VISUAL set to 'nvr'.

Editing a Command Line with Your Preferred Text Editor

Type out this short command, but don't press <CR> just yet:

```
⇒ $ echo "$visual is neat!"
```

Let's say you want to change the text in the string to be all uppercase. You can open the current command line in a text editor by pressing <C-x><C-e> (mnemonic: eXecute Editor). In Vim, you can quickly convert the string to uppercase using the command gUi". Having made that change, save and quit with :wq. The shell executes the command you saved in Neovim:

```
⇒ $ echo "$VISUAL IS NEAT!"
‹ nvim IS NEAT!
```

If you've ever wished that you could use features from Vim while composing or editing a command line, the <C-x><C-e> mapping provides a neat solution.

Mapping edit-command-line in zsh

In bash, the <C-x><C-e> keys are mapped to a function called edit-and-execute-command. In zsh, there's an equivalent function called edit-command-line, which doesn't have a default key mapping. Copy these lines into your .zshrc to bind this function to <C-x><C-e>:

```
autoload -U edit-command-line
zle -N edit-command-line
bindkey '^x^e' edit-command-line
```

Editing a Commit Message with Your Preferred Text Editor

The source code that accompanies this book includes a fresh-project directory. Switch to that directory, then make it into a new Git repository:

```
⇒ $ cd code/fresh-project
⇒ $ rm -rf .git
⇒ $ git init
```

Now stage all the files and commit them:

```
⇒ $ git add .
⇒ $ git commit
```

When you run git commit without any arguments, it opens a text editor so that you can compose a commit message. By default, Git will use the program specified in the $VISUAL environment variable.

Unset git's core.editor Setting

If you've configured the core.editor setting, then Git will use the editor specified there instead of the one specified by the $VISUAL environment variable. You can check the value of this setting by running:

```
⇒ $ git config --system core.editor
⇒ $ git config --global core.editor
❮ vim
⇒ $ git config --local core.editor
❮ vim
```

In this case, the core.editor is set to vim both globally and locally. You can remove these settings using the --unset flag:

```
⇒ $ git config --global --unset core.editor
⇒ $ git config --local --unset core.editor
```

Now Git will use the editor specified by $VISUAL.

Using the Current Neovim Instance as Your Preferred Text Editor

With $VISUAL set to nvim, it's too easy to accidentally start a nested instance of Neovim inside of a terminal buffer. To avoid this situation, you could set $VISUAL to nvr. Put this in your vimrc and reload it:

```
terminal/preferred-editor.vim
if has('nvim') && executable('nvr')
  let $VISUAL="nvr -cc split --remote-wait +'set bufhidden=wipe'"
endif
```

If the nvr executable exists, the $VISUAL environment variable will be set to use that executable. When you run :terminal, the shell inside the terminal buffer will inherit this environment variable.

Here we're using -cc split to open the temporary buffer in a horizontal split window. You could substitute split with vsplit or tabedit to suit your preferences.

The --remote-wait option is important. It instructs nvr to block until the buffer created by the external program is deleted. That means you can't execute any more commands at the command line until the buffer is deleted.

If the temporary buffer was hidden (but not deleted), then nvr would continue to block until that buffer was deleted. This situation can be confusing, but you can prevent this from happening by setting the 'bufhidden' option for the temporary buffer to wipe. This way, hiding the buffer causes it to be automatically deleted.

Now that you've configured $VISUAL to use nvr, try running through the two examples given earlier in this tip: editing a command line and editing a commit message. In both cases, your current Neovim instance will be used as the text editor, which is most convenient. If you combine this with the previous tip, then you should be able to avoid accidentally launching nested instances of Neovim.

CHAPTER 6

Sessions

With Vim's sessions feature you can record the state of your workspace, enabling you to restore that state later on. We'll look at the mechanics of how this works later in this chapter, but first let's consider some scenarios where this functionality could be useful to you.

Make Restarting Vim Frictionless

Suppose you have just discovered a plugin you want to try out. You install the plugin to your $VIMCONFIG/pack/*/start directory. Next, you need to add the directory to your 'runtimepath'. The simplest way to do that is to restart Vim.

Or let's say you've been experimenting with different ways of configuring Vim and something has gone horribly wrong. Maybe the <Tab> key is inserting the wrong kind of whitespace, or the spell checker is stuck in Esperanto. You've lost track of which settings you changed, so you're not sure how to change them back again. Perhaps you could fix the problem by switching Vim off then on again?

The downside to restarting Vim is that you'll lose the state of your workspace. If you only have two or three buffers open, then it won't cause you much trouble to reopen those files one by one after restarting Vim. But if you have a dozen or so buffers open, you might hesitate to restart your editor, especially if you have arranged your workspace into windows and tab pages that help you to focus on your current task. In this scenario, it would be worth your while to record a session before quitting Vim. When resuming Vim, you can then restore that session and pick your work up where you left off.

When used this way, Vim's sessions reduce the friction that might otherwise cause you to hesitate over restarting your editor.

Make Switching Projects Frictionless

Suppose you're working on a task that involves making small changes to lots of different files. You're halfway through the work when something urgent comes up. You need to put down what you're doing, but you know that you'll be coming back to it later (maybe in 30 minutes; maybe next week).

In this scenario, you could save a session to record your workspace in its current state. When you're ready to return to that task, you can reload the session you saved and your workspace will be restored just as you left it.

When used this way, a Vim session represents a project. You might be required to switch context several times in your working day. If you get into the habit of recording Vim sessions, then each time you switch from one project to another, you can pick up where you left off. This continuity can make context-switching less burdensome.

Tip 23

Saving and Restoring Sessions

Sometimes you have to restart Vim. Usually this means losing your list of open buffers, as well as any open tab pages or windows. Fortunately, Vim's session management allows you to save your current workspace so that you can restore it again later.

Saving and Loading Sessions Manually

The source code that accompanies this book includes a webapp directory. Switch to that directory and launch Vim, using the -O flag to open the specified files in vertical splits:

```
$ cd code/webapp
$ vim -O app.js test/app-test.js
```

You should see the app.js and app-test.js files in adjacent windows. Now use the :mksession! command to save the session (:h :mksession):

```
:mksession!
```

Vim records the current session in a Session.vim file in the current working directory. You can restore your workspace to its current state by sourcing

this file. Let's try it out. Use :qa to quit Vim. Then restart Vim using the -S flag
to load your session:

```
$ vim -S
```

Everything should look just as it did when you recorded your session: you
should see the same buffers arranged in the same windows.

The -S flag lets you load a session as you launch Vim. Alternatively, you can
load a session while Vim is running using the :source command (:help :source).
To try this out, use :qa! to quit Vim, then restart Vim without any arguments:

```
$ vim
```

Next, use :source to load the session:

```
:source Session.vim
```

This produces the same result as launching Vim with the -S flag.

By default, the :mksession! command records a Session.vim file in the current
working directory. Also by default, vim -S will look in the current directory for
a Session.vim file to source. In both of these cases, you can provide an argument
to specify the name of a session file. For example, you could use :mksession!
mysession.vim to save a session, and then launch Vim with -S mysession.vim to
restore that session. This way, you could record two or more different sessions
for the same project.

Saving Sessions Automatically

If you like the idea of having your session recorded automatically, you should
try installing the Obsession plugin[1] by Tim Pope. You can install it to your
bundle package like this:

```
$ cd $VIMCONFIG/pack/bundle/start
$ git clone https://github.com/tpope/vim-obsession.git
```

Let's try this out. Start by opening two files, using horizontal splits this time
(just to mix things up):

```
$ vim -o app.js test/app-test.js
```

Now, start tracking your session by running:

```
:Obsession
Tracking session in Session.vim
```

---

1. https://github.com/tpope/vim-obsession

This sets up an autocommand so that the :mksession! command is triggered whenever the VimLeavePre or BufEnter events fire (see Tip 26, *Using Autocommands to Respond to Events*, on page 105). Test this out by opening the package.json file in a new tab page, then quiting Vim:

```
:tabedit package.json
:qa
```

It doesn't matter whether you exit Vim using :q, :qall, ZZ, or whatever, your session should automatically be saved. Now if you restart Vim and load the session, it should pick up from where you left off:

```
$ vim -S
```

Not only does the new session restore buffers, windows, tabs, and so on, it also restores the autocommands that were registered when you ran the :Obsession command. So any changes made to this session will also be recorded when you quit Vim.

You can pause session tracking with the :Obsession command. This works as a toggle, so you can run the same command again to resume tracking later on. If you want to stop tracking your session altogether, run:

```
:Obsession!
```

This removes the Session.vim file and disables the autocommands.

What Does a Session Record?

The 'sessionoptions' option specifies what will be recorded when you save a session (:help 'sessionoptions'). By default, the buffer list is recorded, including buffers that are not currently visible in a window. Buffer names are preserved, but buffer numbers are not. Windows are re-created, preserving the layout and sizing of any splits. Tab pages are restored in the same order, with their windows intact. Your active window and cursor position are also recorded.

Vim 8 has another mechanism for preserving state by means of a viminfo file (:h viminfo-file). In Neovim, this is called the shada file, which is short for *shared data* (:h shada-file). This is where your command-line history, your search history, the contents of registers, and locations of marks are recorded. The feature is enabled by default, so these aspects of state should persist between editing sessions whether or not you load a session file.

When you restart Vim, you typically lose your undo history. Neither sessions nor viminfo will help you here, but Vim's persistent undo feature handles this. Read the next tip to learn more.

Tip 24

Making Undo Persist Between Sessions

The undo command is a lifesaver when you need to revert changes that didn't work out. Typically, you can only undo changes that were made to a file during the current editing session. By enabling Vim's 'undofile' option, you can make undo history persist between editing sessions.

Open the green-bottles.txt file from the source code that accompanies this book in Vim:

green-bottles.txt

```
10 green bottles hanging on the wall.
```

Use the `<C-x>` command to decrement the number at the start of the line. Now you can use u to undo the change and `<C-r>` to redo it. If you quit Vim and then reopen the same file, what do you expect to happen when you use the u command?

Your undo history is usually lost when you quit your text editor. If you enable the 'undofile' option, then Vim will write your undo history to a hidden file, making it persist between editing sessions (:help persistent-undo). To enable this feature, add this line to your vimrc file then reload it:

```
set undofile
```

Switch back to the green-bottles.txt file and use the `<C-x>` command again to decrement, then for good measure, use . a couple of times to repeat the change. Now quit Vim and reopen the same file. You should be able to use u to undo those changes. Pretty cool, huh?

Saving Undo Files in a Designated Directory

With the 'undofile' option enabled, Vim records the undo history for a file by writing to a hidden file in the same directory. In the previous example, the green-bottles.txt file would have its undo history written to a file called .green-bottles.txt.un~. This can lead to a proliferation of hidden files mixed into your working directory.

To avoid this, use the 'undodir' option to specify a directory where your undo files will be saved. Add this line to your vimrc, then reload your vimrc:

```
set undodir=$VIMDATA/undo
```

If the path specified in 'undodir' doesn't exist, then persistent undo won't work. Create the directory by running:

⇒ `:call mkdir(&undodir, 'p')`

If you're using Neovim, you can stick with the default 'undodir' value of $XDG_DATA_HOME/nvim/undo. You'll still have to create the directory, though.

Disabling Persistent Undo for Temporary Files

Persistent undo is an appealing feature, but it brings some security concerns. Suppose you are using a password manager that uses $VISUAL to launch your preferred text editor. You wouldn't want to leak your secure password in the form of a hidden undo file.

To avoid this situation, use an autocommand to disable 'undofile' locally for files that match a particular pattern. For example, here's how to disable persistent undo for all files in the /tmp directory:

forget-undo-in-tmpfile.vim
```
augroup vimrc
  autocmd!
  autocmd BufWritePre /tmp/* setlocal noundofile
augroup END
```

You can tweak the file pattern to suit your needs. If you are not familiar with Vim's autocommands, read Tip 26, *Using Autocommands to Respond to Events*, on page 105 for an introduction.

Putting It All Together

Copy this snippet into your vimrc whether you're using Vim or Neovim:

persistent-undo/universal.vim
```
set undofile
if !has('nvim')
  set undodir=~/.vim/undo
endif
augroup vimrc
  autocmd!
  autocmd BufWritePre /tmp/* setlocal noundofile
augroup END
```

This enables persistent undo (except for temporary files) and saves undo files to a designated directory.

Tip 25

Restarting Terminal Processes When Resuming a Session

 Neovim only

If you're running Neovim, you might also want your session file to record details of which processes were running in terminal buffers. By taking care to name your terminal buffers appropriately, you can make your processes resume when you restore a session.

Preparation

The source code that accompanies this book includes a webapp directory. Switch to that directory and install the dependencies:

```
$ cd code/webapp
$ npm install
```

This directory contains a simple web server. You can start the server by running:

```
$ npm run server
```

You'll also find a small test suite, which you can run with:

```
$ npm run test
```

We'll use these commands to illustrate the examples in this tip, so make sure you can run them before you proceed.

Saving a Session Captures Terminal Buffers by Name

To get started, open the app.js file in Neovim:

```
$ nvim app.js
```

Now you're going to use two slightly different methods to start the webserver. First, open a new terminal buffer in a split:

```
:split | terminal
```

Press i to activate Terminal mode, then start the webserver on port 3001:

```
» PORT=3001 npm run server
```

Next, you'll start a second webserver on port 3002 with this one-liner:

⇒ `:split | terminal PORT=3002 npm run server`

Side by side, the two terminal buffers look similar. There's one significant difference I want to draw your attention to: the buffer names. You can list them by running:

⇒ `:ls`
⟨ ```
1   a   "app.js"   line 1
2 #a-   "term://.//76529:/usr/local/bin/bash" line 9
3 %a-   "term://.//76606:PORT=3002 npm run server" line 6
```

These can be generalized as term://{cwd}//{pid}:{cmd}. We can ignore the {cwd} and {pid}, but the {cmd} is significant. In one terminal buffer, the {cmd} is /usr/local/bin/bash, while in the other one it's PORT=3002 npm run server.

Save the current session then quit:

⇒ `:mksession!`
⇒ `:qa!`

Then, restart Neovim using the -S flag to restore the session you just recorded:

⇒ `$ nvim -S`

You should now see two terminal buffers: one containing a webserver process, and the other containing a bash shell. This doesn't faithfully reproduce the session you recorded, which had two webserver processes running side by side. So what's going on here?

When you save a session, the name of each buffer is recorded. In one case, you used :terminal PORT=3002 npm run server to launch the webserver process directly. When the session was restored, Neovim re-created this buffer by running: :edit term://PORT=3002 npm run server, which restarts the webserver process.

In the other case, you used :terminal to start a bash shell, then ran the npm run server command inside of the shell to launch the webserver. When the session was restored, Neovim re-created this buffer by running :edit term:///usr/local/bin/bash, which restarts the bash shell. Commands that were entered in the shell are not recorded in the session, although you may be able to retrieve them from your bash history.

Generally speaking, if you start a process using :terminal {cmd}, the {cmd} process will be restarted when a session is restored. Whereas if you use :terminal to start a shell, restoring your session will restore the shell. It doesn't matter
```

what commands you executed in the original shell; they won't be recorded as part of a Vim session.

Renaming a Terminal Buffer

When it comes to saving and restoring sessions, the name of a terminal buffer is significant. You'll be pleased to learn that you can change the name of a terminal buffer after creating it. To see how this works, let's set up a new scenario. Open the app.js and test/app-test.js files, each in their own tab pages:

⇒ `$ nvim -p app.js test/app-test.js`

In the first tab page, create a new terminal:

⇒ `:split | terminal`

Then switch to Terminal mode and run:

⇒ `» PORT=3001 npm run server`

Switch to the next tab and create a new terminal there:

⇒ `:tabnext`
⇒ `:split | terminal`

Then switch to Terminal mode and run:

⇒ `» PORT=3002 npm run test:watch`

Now take a look at the buffer names:

⇒ `:ls`
❮
```
  1  a   "app.js"                      line 1
  2 #a   "test/app-test.js"            line 1
  3  a-  "term://.//78008:/usr/local/bin/bash" line 0
  4 %a-  "term://.//78095:/usr/local/bin/bash" line 18
```

You already know what would happen if you were to save your session now and restore it: you would end up with two terminal buffers, each running a bash shell. It would be better if restoring a session would cause both the webserver and the test runner processes to start up again. Let's make it so.

You can use the :file {name} command to rename your terminal buffers (:help :file_f). Activate the window containing the webserver, then run:

⇒ `:file term://PORT=3001 npm run server`

Next, activate the window containing the test runner and run:

⇒ `:file term://PORT=3002 npm run test:watch`

Inspect the buffer list to check that it's worked, then record your session and quit Neovim:

```
:ls
  1  a    "app.js"                              line 1
  2 #a    "test/app-test.js"                    line 1
  3  a-   "term://PORT=3001 npm run server" line 0
  4 %a-   "term://PORT=3002 npm run test:watch" line 18
:mksession!
:qa!
```

Now, restart Neovim and load the session you just recorded:

```
$ nvim -S
```

You should find that both the webserver and the test runner processes have been restarted.

Configuring Vim

You can configure Vim by setting options in your vimrc file. This file is sourced when Vim starts up, so any options you set there will be applied each time you launch Vim. This mechanism works fine for setting global options—the settings you want to apply throughout Vim. But sometimes you need to tweak your settings for different contexts. Perhaps you want to customize a setting one way for JavaScript files and another way for JSON files. Perhaps your personal preference is to always use two spaces for indentation, but you collaborate on some projects where tabs are preferred. In this chapter, you'll discover a few different mechanisms you can use for applying settings in a particular context.

Tip 26

Using Autocommands to Respond to Events

This tip comes in two parts. In the first part, you'll try out some examples of autocommands to understand how they work. In the second part, you'll look at some real examples of how autocommands can be useful, collected from other tips in this book.

Understanding Autocommands

Here's a short sample Vim script that defines two autocommands:

autocmd-demo/autocmds-01.vim
```
augroup demo
  autocmd!
  autocmd BufReadPost * echo 'Reading: ' . expand('<afile>')
  autocmd BufWritePost * echo 'Writing: ' . expand('<afile>')
augroup END
```

Before we look at the syntax of these autocommands, let's see how they behave. Open that script in a fresh instance of Vim:

```
⇒  $ cd code/autocmd-demo/
⇒  $ vim autocmds-01.vim
```

Then source the file:

```
⇒  :source %
```

Now, Vim prints a message each time you read or write a file:

```
⇒  :edit!
‹  Reading: autocmds-01.vim
⇒  :write
‹  Writing: autocmds-01.vim
⇒  :edit! $MYVIMRC
‹  Reading: ~/.vim/vimrc
```

For this demo, you'll want to use the :edit! variant (note the trailing bang). This always reads the file into a buffer, triggering the BufReadPost event. By contrast, the bang-less :edit command won't trigger that event if the file has already been read into a buffer. (:h :edit!)

Now, let's consider how these autocommands work. The general format for defining an autocommand looks like this (:help :autocmd):

```
autocmd {event} {pattern} {cmd}
```

Let's compare the first of our autocommands with this general format. The {event} is BufReadPost, the {pattern} is *, and everything after the pattern is the {cmd}.

In the {cmd}, the <afile> item stands for the name of the current file. This special item is only defined while the autocommand is executing. (You'll get a blank line if you run :echo expand('<afile>') by hand at Vim's command line.) Other special items available in this context include <abuf> and <amatch> (:help <afile>).

Vim fires the BufReadPost command after reading a file into a buffer (:h BufRead-Post). If the buffer's filepath matches the pattern defined in our autocommand, then Vim executes the specified {cmd}. Since we're using the * wildcard here, this autocommand executes for all buffers.

Let's experiment with changing the {pattern} field to be more selective. This short script defines an autocommand that fires whenever you read a Vim script file:

```
autocmd-demo/autocmds-02.vim
augroup demo
  autocmd!
  autocmd BufReadPost *.vim,vimrc
       \ echo 'Editing Vim script: ' . expand('<afile>')
augroup END
```

As before, the {event} is BufReadPost, but this time the {pattern} is designed to match any Vim script file. Most Vim script files use the .vim extension, but the vimrc file is a special case. When defining an autocommand, you can specify one or more patterns using commas to separate each one (:h autocmd-patterns).

To try out this autocommand, source the script:

⇒ `:source autocmds-02.vim`

Now, you'll see the Editing Vim script message when you open a .vim or vimrc file:

⇒ `:edit! autocmds-02.vim`
‹ `Editing Vim script: autocmds-02.vim`
⇒ `:edit! $MYVIMRC`
‹ `Editing Vim script: ~/.vim/vimrc`

But no message is logged when you open a readme.md file:

⇒ `:edit! readme.md`

If you're paying close attention, you might wonder why you didn't see the Reading: ... message from the autocommand defined earlier. Hold that thought —we'll come back to that a little bit later.

It looks like we've created an autocommand that detects Vim script files. But watch what happens if you create a new file with the .vim extension:

⇒ `:new example.vim`

Vim didn't print any message this time. Why not? Because our autocommand listens for the BufReadPost event, which fires only after a buffer is read from a file on disk. When you use the :new {filename} command, Vim creates the buffer in memory, but until you :write, the buffer has no corresponding file on disk.

You can use another one of Vim's events to handle this case: BufNewFile (:h BufNewFile). This next Vim script refines the previous autocommand to listen for both events:

```
autocmd-demo/autocmds-03.vim
augroup demo
  autocmd!
  autocmd BufNewFile,BufReadPost vimrc,*.vim
      \ echo 'Editing Vim script: ' . expand('<afile>')
augroup END
```

After sourcing this script, you can create a new Vim script file and the auto-command fires:

⇒ `:source autocmds-03.vim`
⇒ `:new example2.vim`
❮ `Editing Vim script: example2.vim`

To get the desired behavior, you may sometimes need to use more than one event to trigger an autocommand. Other times, you may find that there's another event more suitable. For this particular case, you could produce a similar result by listening instead for the FileType event (:h FileType):

```
autocmd-demo/autocmds-04.vim
augroup demo
  autocmd!
  autocmd FileType vim
      \ echo 'Editing Vim script: ' . expand('<afile>') . '\n'
      \ . 'Filetype: '. expand('<amatch>')
augroup END
```

To see this autocommand in action, source the file:

⇒ `:source autocmds-04.vim`

As before, you'll see the Editing Vim script... message when you open a Vim script file. This autocommand is triggered whenever you change the 'filetype' setting. It doesn't matter how the file is named, as the following example demonstrates:

⇒ `:edit! readme.md`
⇒ `:set filetype?`
❮ `markdown`
⇒ `:set filetype=vim`
❮ `Editing Vim script: readme.md`
`Filetype: vim`

For most {event}s, the {pattern} is tested against the filename of the active buffer. The FileType event is different. Here, the {pattern} is matched against the filetype. In this example, if the filetype is vim, the autocommand fires.

For events such as FileType where the treatment of {pattern} deviates from normal, Vim's documentation describes the behavior. For more examples, check the documentation for :h Syntax, :h OptionSet, and :h QuickFixCmdPre. If the documentation for an event doesn't mention what the {pattern} is matched against, you can assume it's tested against the filename of the active buffer.

Browsing Events

You've already seen the BufNewFile and BufReadPost events in action. It's probably no surprise to learn that Vim also has a BufReadPre event, which fires *before* reading a file into a buffer. Vim's events typically offer this level of granularity, which means you can make your autocommand fire at just the right moment.

There are events for all sorts of occasions. You can listen for events each time you read or write a file; you can create a new buffer, window, or tab page (BufNew, WinNew, TabNew); you can launch or quit Vim (VimEnter, VimLeave); change text or move the cursor (TextChanged, CursorMoved). To see an overview of all Vim's events, look up :help {event}. Whatever you want to do with an autocommand, it's likely Vim has one or more events you can hook into.

If you're trying to achieve something that can't be done with Vim's events, be assured that this is an area of activity in Vim's development. For example, the TextYankPost event was added recently (Vim 8.0.1206 and Neovim 0.1.3), as were the CmdlineEnter and CmdlineLeave events (Vim 8.0.1401 and Neovim 0.2.3). If you want to see more events added, get involved with Vim or Neovim.

Tearing Down Autocommands

This next Vim script is almost identical to the first example, with one significant change:

```
autocmd-demo/autocmds-05.vim
augroup demo
  autocmd BufReadPost * echo 'Reading: ' . expand('<afile>')
  autocmd BufWritePost * echo 'Writing: ' . expand('<afile>')
augroup END
```

Can you spot the difference? The first script called autocmd!, but that line is missing from this script. Let's see how this changes the behavior of the autocommands. Open that script in a fresh instance of Vim:

```
$ cd code/autocmds-demo/
$ vim autocmds-05.vim
```

Source the file, then use the :edit! command to trigger an autocommand:

```
:source %
:edit!
« Reading: autocmds-05.vim
```

No surprises so far. But watch what happens if you source the file a second time:

```
⇒ :source %
⇒ :edit!
❮ Reading: autocmds-05.vim
  Reading: autocmds-05.vim
```

The message gets logged twice. If you were to source the file a third time, the message would get logged three times each time you trigger the BufReadPost event, and so on. Each time you source that script, Vim adds the specified autocommands, but it doesn't remove any existing autocommands. As a result, you end up with multiple autocommands defined for the same {event} and {pattern}.

You can inspect the autocommands in the demo group:

```
⇒ :autocmd demo
❮ --- Autocommands ---
  demo  BufRead
      *            echo 'Reading: ' . expand('<afile>')
                   echo 'Reading: ' . expand('<afile>')
  demo  BufWritePost
      *            echo 'Writing: ' . expand('<afile>')
                   echo 'Writing: ' . expand('<afile>')
```

That reveals the duplicate autocommands. You can remove autocommands using the :autocmd! command (:help autocommand-remove). Since all of these autocommands were defined inside the demo group, you can remove them all together by running:

```
⇒ :autocmd! demo
⇒ :autocmd demo
❮ --- Autocommands ---
```

Ideally, you don't want to be calling that manually. Instead, it's best to define your autocommands in such a way that they are cleanly removed each time they are sourced. Use this template as a starting point:

```
augroup unique_group_name
  autocmd!
  " Define autocommands here:
augroup END
```

This ensures you don't accidentally create multiple autocommands for the same {event} and {pattern}.

Autocommands in Use

The autocommands discussed in this section are taken from other tips in this book. For the sake of brevity, each autocommand is presented without the containing group.

Using BufWritePre to Selectively Disable Persistent Undo

In *Disabling Persistent Undo for Temporary Files*, on page 100, we use this autocommand:

```
autocmd BufWritePre /tmp/* setlocal noundofile
```

The {cmd} disables the 'undofile' option. The BufWritePre event is triggered just before the file is written, and the autocommand is only executed if the file matches the {pattern}: /tmp/*.

Responding to User-Defined Events

In *Setting Local Variables for Files in a Project*, on page 119, we use this autocommand:

```
autocmd User ProjectionistActivate call s:linters()
```

This autocommand is triggered by the User event, with ProjectionistActivate as the pattern. The User event is special in the sense that Vim never fires it automatically, but you can trigger an event like this one yourself:

⇒ `:doautocmd User ProjectionistActivate`

Looking at this example, you might be wondering: Why would I do that? Why not just run :call s:linters() directly? Plugins can use this mechanism to create their own events.

In the case of Projectionist, the plugin configures itself by listening for various different native events. The FileType and VimEnter events both cause Projectionist to do similar work in slightly different ways. In both cases, the User Projectionist-Detect event gets called. Triggering this event means that the user can use this event, instead of listening for the FileType and VimEnter events.

Tip 27

Respecting Project Conventions

When working on multiple codebases, you may encounter different conventions for indentation size, indentation style, character encodings, and so on. The .editorconfig file has become a de-facto standard for specifying settings, scoped by filetype and directory. This format is designed to be editor-agnostic, and you can make Vim understand these files by installing a plugin.

Preparation

In this tip, you'll use the vim-editorconfig plugin[1] by sgur. You can install it to your bundle package like this:

```
$ cd $VIMCONFIG/pack/bundle/start
$ git clone https://github.com/sgur/vim-editorconfig.git
```

Specifying Your Personal Preferences

You can set your personal preferences by creating an .editorconfig file in your home directory. Use this example as a starting point (you can always customize it later):

```
.editorconfig
root = true

[*]
end_of_line = lf
charset = utf-8

[*.{js,json}]
indent_style = space
indent_size = 2

[Makefile]
indent_style = tab
```

The EditorConfig file format consists of *sections* and *properties*. The lines containing a filename or glob in square brackets mark the beginning of a section. Within a section, you can assign a property with a value. For details of the file format, check the EditorConfig documentation.[2]

---

1. https://github.com/sgur/vim-editorconfig
2. http://editorconfig.org/#file-format-details

Which EditorConfig Plugin to Use?

I know of two different plugins that add EditorConfig support to Vim. The *official* plugin is published on GitHub under the EditorConfig organization and is named editorconfig-vim.[a] This plugin is implemented using Python, so to use it with Vim 8, you must have the +python feature enabled; to use it with Neovim, you must install the Python provider (see Tip 3, *Enabling Python Support in Neovim*, on page 7). The alternative is a plugin named vim-editorconfig,[b] which is implemented in pure Vim script.

Both plugins work well and you can use whichever one you prefer. (Just make sure you don't install both at once!) In this tip, I recommend using the pure Vim script implementation because it doesn't require Python, and therefore, is slightly easier to install. If you're already using the official editorconfig-vim plugin and it works for you, there's no need to change.

---

a. https://github.com/editorconfig/editorconfig-vim
b. https://github.com/sgur/vim-editorconfig

The root property is unusual in that it must be declared at the top of the config file before the first section. We'll discuss the root property in more detail later in this tip.

The first section uses the * wildcard. The end_of_line property controls how line breaks are represented, while the charset property specifies the character set. In Vim, these properties roughly correspond to the 'fileformat' and 'fileencoding' options.

The next section configures .js and .json files to use two spaces for indentation. In Vim, these settings are controlled by the 'expandtab' and 'shiftwidth' options.

Let's create a new JavaScript file called demo.js and inspect the relevant settings:

```
:edit demo.js
:set expandtab? shiftwidth?
  expandtab
  shiftwidth=2
:set fileformat? fileencoding?
  fileformat=unix
  fileencoding=utf-8
```

The 'expandtab' and 'shiftwidth' options are configured to use two spaces for indentation, which demonstrates that the settings from the *.js section have been applied. And the 'fileformat' and 'fileencoding' options are correctly configured, which demonstrates that the settings from the * section have also been applied.

The final section of the .editorconfig file configures Makefiles to use tab characters for indentation. Now, let's open a Makefile (or create a new one) and inspect its indentation settings:

```
:edit Makefile
:set expandtab? shiftwidth?
noexpandtab
  shiftwidth=8
:set fileformat? fileencoding?
  fileformat=unix
  fileencoding=utf-8
```

This time, the 'expandtab' option is disabled, and 'shiftwidth' uses Vim's default value of 8. The 'fileformat' and 'fileencoding' options are set as before.

When you put an .editorconfig file in your home directory, the settings you specify there will apply to any file in your home directory or below. That means your ~/.editorconfig file is a good place to set your personal preferences. Next, let's consider the case where you're working on a project that diverges from your usual coding style.

Specifying Your Project Preferences

The source code that accompanies this book includes two minimal projects that follow different indentation styles. Open both projects in Vim:

```
$ cd code
$ vim -o spacewalk/index.js taboo/index.js
```

If you check the indentation settings for either buffer, you'll see the same values:

```
:set expandtab? shiftwidth?
  expandtab
  shiftwidth=2
```

These settings are coming from the .editorconfig file in your home directory. It would be helpful to be able to see the tab characters, so enable the 'list' option for each window:

```
:windo set list
```

Now, you should be able to see that the spacewalk/index.js file uses two spaces for indentation, whereas the taboo/index.js file uses tabs. If you try adding a new line of code to each of those files, you'll find that Vim uses two spaces for indentation. That's fine for the spacewalk project, but not okay for taboo.

You can fix this by adding a project-specific .editorconfig file. Create a taboo/ .editorconfig file containing the following:

```
taboo-editorconfig
[*.{js,json}]
indent_style = tab
indent_size = 4
```

To apply these settings, reload the taboo/index.js buffer:

```
:b taboo/index.js
:edit!
:set expandtab? shiftwidth?
noexpandtab
  shiftwidth=4
```

Now, the 'expandtab' and 'shiftwidth' settings use the properties specified in the project's .editorconfig file.

Editorconfig Precedence

When you open a file, the EditorConfig plugin looks in that file's directory for an .editorconfig file. It then checks for an .editorconfig file in the parent directory, and the grandparent directory, and so on. Having located one or more config files, the plugin then applies the settings specified in each one, starting at the top and working down to the bottom. The closest .editorconfig file is applied last, so any settings specified there will override the settings from above.

You can modify this behavior using the root property. When the EditorConfig plugin finds a config file where root is set to true, it stops searching upward for config files. If you have an .editorconfig file in your home directory, I recommend using root=true there. For project-level .editorconfig files, the root property is optional. In either case, if you use root=true in an .editorconfig file, I recommend specifying a value for all supported properties, since they won't be inherited from ancestor configuration files.

Most programmers' text editors support the EditorConfig format, either natively or via a plugin. So when you publish a project, it's a good idea to include your .editorconfig file in source control. Anyone who downloads your source code will receive the settings you specified. This way, you're much less likely to receive patches that diverge from your project's formatting conventions.

In the previous demonstration, you created a .editorconfig file to specify settings for the taboo directory. For the sake of consistency, you could also create a .editorconfig file for the spacewalk directory. This would duplicate some of the settings from the .editorconfig file in your home directory, but the two files serve different purposes. Your root .editorconfig file sets your personal preferences (for projects without their own config file), while the project .editorconfig file specifies project-level preferences.

Supported Properties

By design, the editorconfig file format is not tied to any particular text editor. For each of the supported properties, you can make an educated guess as to what it's supposed to do, but the implementation details will vary between text editors. The following table shows which Vim settings are influenced by the EditorConfig properties:

EditorConfig property	Corresponding Vim option(s)
charset	'fileencoding' and 'bomb'
end_of_line	'fileformat'
indent_size	'shiftwidth'
indent_style	'expandtab'
tab_width	'tabstop'
insert_final_newline	'fixendofline'
max_line_length	'textwidth'
trim_trailing_whitespace	Implemented as an autocommand

If you want to know more about any of those Vim options, you can look them up via the :help command.

Note that the settings applied by the EditorConfig plugin will take precedence over any settings you apply in your vimrc file.

Tip 28

Setting Buffer-Local Configuration Per Project

Autocommands and ftplugins allow you to apply settings to all files of a particular filetype. But what if you want to apply settings to files within a directory? Vim doesn't have a built-in mechanism for this, but you can achieve this effect using the Projectionist plugin.

Preparation

In this tip, you'll use two plugins: Projectionist by Tim Pope,[3] and ALE by Andrew Wray.[4] You can install these to your bundle package like this:

```
⇒ $ cd $VIMCONFIG/pack/bundle/start
⇒ $ git clone https://github.com/tpope/vim-projectionist.git
⇒ $ git clone https://github.com/w0rp/ale.git
```

Run :helptags ALL to index the documentation for these plugins.

The Projectionist plugin is the main subject here, while the ALE plugin is merely used for illustrative purposes. Check out Tip 12, *Linting the Current File*, on page 50 for details on how the ALE plugin works.

Setting Up the Demo Projects

You'll use two different projects as you work through this tip. Both are simple JavaScript projects, but each one is configured to use a different linting tool. The linting project uses eslint, whereas the hinting project uses jshint. You'll need to install the dependencies for each project.

First, change to the linting directory and install its dependencies. Then run eslint to check that it works:

```
⇒ $ cd code/linting
⇒ $ npm install
❮ date-in@1.0.0 /Users/drew/modvim/code/linting
  └── eslint@3.19.0

⇒ $ ./node_modules/.bin/eslint date-in.js
❮  1:33  error  Strings must use doublequote  quotes
   7:5   error  'offset' is constant          no-const-assign
   9:5   error  'offset' is constant          no-const-assign
  13:47  error  Missing semicolon             semi

  ✖ 4 problems (4 errors, 0 warnings)
```

Next, do the same for the hinting project:

```
⇒ $ cd code/hinting
⇒ $ npm install
❮ date-in@1.0.0 /Users/drew/modvim/code/hinting
  └── jshint@2.9.5
⇒ $ ./node_modules/.bin/jshint date-in.js
❮ date-in.js: line 15, col 47, Missing semicolon.

  1 error
```

3. https://github.com/tpope/vim-projectionist
4. https://github.com/w0rp/ale

Add the following lines to your vimrc:

ale-config/linters.vim
```
let g:ale_linters = {
\   'javascript': ['eslint'],
\ }
```

This makes ALE use eslint for JavaScript files.

Configuring ALE Globally and Locally

The ALE plugin automatically lints the current buffer. For JavaScript files, ALE supports many linting tools, including eslint and jshint. In preparation for this tip, you set the g:ale_linters variable, making ALE use eslint for all JavaScript files. That's exactly the behavior we want for the linting project. But we're going to have to find a way to override this preference for the hinting project.

In both linting and hinting projects, you'll find a file called date-in.js. Open both files using one tab page for each project:

⇒ **$ cd code**
⇒ **$ vim -p linting/date-in.js hinting/date-in.js**

Use :tabfirst to activate the linting project and :tablast to activate the hinting project.

You can get details about how ALE is configured for the current file using the :ALEInfo command. At present, running this command in either project will print the same information:

⇒ **:ALEInfo**
❮ Current Filetype: javascript
Available Linters: ['eslint', 'flow', 'jscs', 'jshint', 'standard', 'xo']
  Enabled Linters: ['eslint']
...

In both cases, the current filetype is JavaScript and the only enabled linter is eslint.

Activate the hinting project, then set the b:ale_linters variable as follows:

⇒ **:tablast**
⇒ **:let b:ale_linters = {'javascript': ['jshint']}**
⇒ **:ALEInfo**
❮ Current Filetype: javascript
Available Linters: ['eslint', 'flow', 'jscs', 'jshint', 'standard', 'xo']
  Enabled Linters: ['jshint']
...

For the hinting/date-in.js file, ALE now uses jshint instead of eslint. That's because ALE gives higher precedence to the buffer-local b:ale_linters variable than the global g:ale_linters equivalent. The linting/date-in.js file does not have b:ale_linters set, so it still uses the global setting.

Now, we have the behavior we want: ALE defaults to using eslint for JavaScript files, but it uses jshint where specified. Next, let's find a way to automate this so that we don't have to set b:ale_linters by hand.

Setting Local Variables for Files in a Project

Vim provides a couple of mechanisms that allow you to apply settings by filetype: either by creating a filetype plugin or by using autocmds (as discussed in Tip 26, *Using Autocommands to Respond to Events*, on page 105). Those methods won't help in this case, because we want to apply different settings to two different files with the same filetype.

Another way to approach this problem is to say that we want to apply different settings for each *project*. That's where the Projectionist plugin can help. By placing a .projections.json file in the root directory of your project, you can make Projectionist apply customizations that only affect the files contained in that directory. The JSON format allows you to specify a filepath or glob, then attach metadata to any buffers that match that pattern.

In the hinting directory, create a .projections.json file with the following contents:

ale-config/projections.json
```
{
  "*.js": {
    "linters": ["jshint"]
  }
}
```

If you open any file in the hinting directory, the metadata specified in the .projections.json file will be attached to the buffer by means of a variable called b:projectionist.

When you started your current Vim session, the .projections.json file didn't exist, so the b:projectionist variable isn't currently set on any of your buffers. To fix this, you can either restart Vim or use the :edit! command to reload your existing buffers. (If you choose to restart Vim you might want to record a session first. See Tip 23, *Saving and Restoring Sessions*, on page 96 to find out how.) Next, inspect the b:projectionist variable on the hinting/date-in.js file:

⇒ `:bufdo edit!`
⇒ `:edit hinting/date-in.js`
⇒ `:echo b:projectionist`

```
❮ {
    '/Users/drew/modvim/code/hinting': [
      {'*.js': {'linters': ['jshint']}}
    ]
  }
```

You can use the projectionst#query(key) function to retrieve metadata for a specified key. This function takes the filepath of the active buffer into account.
When the active buffer is hinting/package.json or linting/date-in.js, a query for the
'linters' key returns an empty list:

```
⇒ :edit hinting/package.json
⇒ :echo projectionist#query('linters')
❮ []
⇒ :edit linting/date-in.js
⇒ :echo projectionist#query('linters')
❮ []
```

In the case of hinting/package.json, the b:projectionist metadata is available, but the
filepath doesn't match the *.js pattern. Whereas the linting/date-in.js file is in a
different directory entirely, so your projectionst configuration doesn't even
apply there.

When the hinting/date-in.js buffer is active and you query for the 'linters' key, you
get a result (here and in later examples, I've pretty-printed the output from
:echo to make it fit the page):

```
⇒ :edit hinting/date-in.js
⇒ :echo projectionist#query('linters')
❮ [
    ['/Users/drew/modvim/code/hinting', ['jshint']]
  ]
```

The list contains one result: itself a list of the form [root, value]. The root is the
directory where the .projections.json file is defined (we will explore the signifi-
cance of this in the next section). The value of ['jshint'] is the part that we are
interested in.

Remember what we're trying to achieve here: we want to define a local
b:ale_linters variable so that all JavaScript files in the hinting directory use jshint.
What we've done so far is define a projection that matches .js files, and
attaches metadata to those buffers with the 'linters' key. Next, we want to define
a b:ale_linters variable for any buffers that have the 'linters' metadata attached.

Copy this snippet of Vim script into your vimrc file and reload it:

```
ale-config/project-config.vim
augroup configure_projects
  autocmd!
  autocmd User ProjectionistActivate call s:linters()
augroup END

function! s:linters() abort
  let l:linters = projectionist#query('linters')
  if len(l:linters) > 0
    let b:ale_linters = {&filetype: l:linters[0][1]}
  endif
endfunction
```

The ProjectionistActivate autocommand lets you run code after Projectionist has attached metadata to a buffer. Here, the autocommand triggers the s:linters() function, which queries for the 'linters' key. If the active buffer has a value for that key, then b:ale_linters is set to a dictionary, associating the current filetype with the specified linters.

Use :qa! to quit Vim, then open the two date-in.js files again in two separate tabs:

⇒ **$ vim -p linting/date-in.js hinting/date-in.js**

When the linting/date-in.js is active, ALE uses eslint. But when the hinting/date-in.js is active, ALE uses jshint:

⇒ **:tabfirst**
⇒ **:ALEInfo**
❮ Enabled Linters: ['eslint']
⇒ **:tablast**
⇒ **:ALEInfo**
❮ Enabled Linters: ['jshint']

That's just what we wanted!

Projectionist Specificity

Metadata that you specify in a projections.json file will be attached to all files beneath that directory. You can place a .projections.json configuration file in more than one directory, which means it's possible for a file to have metadata attached to it from more than one set of projections.

Let's explore this idea. Switch to the code/hardwrap directory:

⇒ **$ cd code/hardwrap**

This directory contains a couple of plaintext files and a couple of Markdown files, each containing pseudo-Latin placeholder text:

```
hardwrap
├── .projections.json
├── lorem-ipsum.md
├── pellentesque.txt
└── subdir
    ├── .projections.json
    ├── maecenas.txt
    └── vestibulum.md
```

In the project root, you'll find a .projections.json file containing the following:

hardwrap/.projections.json
```
{
  "*": { "hardwrap": "78" }
}
```

The "*" pattern matches all files within the hardwrap directory, as well as all files in any subdirectories. Open the lorem-ipsum.md file and query Projectionist for the 'hardwrap' key:

```
:edit lorem-ipsum.md
:echo projectionist#query('hardwrap')
[
    ['/Users/drew/modvim/code/hardwrap', '78']
]
```

If you run the same query in the pellentesque.txt and subdir/vestibulum.md files, you'll see the same output.

In the subdir directory, you'll find another .projections.json file containing the following:

hardwrap/subdir/.projections.json
```
{
  "*.txt": { "hardwrap": "42" }
}
```

This pattern only matches files with the .txt extension. Open the subdir/maecenas.txt file and query Projectionist for the 'hardwrap' key:

```
:edit subdir/maecenas.txt
:echo projectionist#query('hardwrap')
[
    ['/Users/drew/modvim/code/hardwrap/subdir', '42'],
    ['/Users/drew/modvim/code/hardwrap', '78']
]
```

This time the list of matches contains two results: one from each .projections.json file. The proximity between the current buffer and the Projections config file determines the order of the results.

Suppose you want to use the value of 'hardwrap' for Vim's 'textwidth' setting. You can either use the value 42 or 78, but not both! It would make sense here to use the value from the .projections.json file closest to the current buffer, which is the first result from the query.

This snippet of Vim script would do the trick:

```
hardwrap.vim
augroup configure_projects
  autocmd!
  autocmd User ProjectionistActivate call s:hardwrap()
augroup END

function! s:hardwrap() abort
  for [root, value] in projectionist#query('hardwrap')
    let &l:textwidth = value
    break
  endfor
endfunction
```

The ProjectionistActivate autocommand triggers the s:hardwrap() function. This queries Projectionist for the 'hardwrap' key, then loops through the results and uses the matching value to set the buffer-local 'textwidth' option. The break statement causes the loop to exit after its first execution. The outcome is that the first result from the query is used, while any subsequent results are discarded. (Taking out the break statement would make the last item in the list stick.)

Designing Generalized Projections

In the first example, you used the key 'linters' to attach data that would be used to set the b:ale_linters variable. In the second example, you used the key 'hardwrap' to set the 'textwidth' option. You might wonder: Why not rename the 'linters' key to 'ale_linters', and the 'hardwrap' key to 'textwidth'? That would give a more accurate description of how the metadata is being used.

You can do that if you like, but you might regret it later when you switch from ALE to another linting plugin. In that scenario, you could adapt the s:linters() function in your vimrc, so that instead of setting the b:ale_linters variable, it would do something equivalent for your preferred linting plugin. Using a generic key such as 'linters' makes it easy to imagine other ways the metadata could be used.

Projections are defined in a .json file. That means you can safely check them into source control, just like an .editorconfig file. By contrast, a Vim script file can be executed, making it a potential security risk. See *What About Local vimrc Files?*, on page 124.

The .projections.json file format is editor-agnostic. In theory, you could use it to configure any text editor or tooling. I can't name any other text editors that use projections today, but it's a useful format and it might spread beyond the Vim ecosystem. When defining projections, I prefer to use keys that are abstract, rather than choosing keys that are tightly coupled to Vim's options or to a particular plugin.

> ## What About Local vimrc Files?
>
> Enabling the 'exrc' option (:help 'exrc') changes Vim's behavior on start up: after sourcing the vimrc file in your home directory, Vim will source the vimrc file in your *current working directory*, if such a file is present. Using this feature, you could create a local vimrc file that customizes Vim's behavior for a particular project. That idea might seem appealing, but you should be aware of the security risks.
>
> Imagine checking out an open source project that contained a hidden .vimrc. If you have 'exrc' enabled, that Vim script file would be automatically sourced when you started Vim from the project's home directory. ("Hello, I'm an autocmd. Let me silently run system(rm -rf /) for you..."). You can protect yourself in this scenario by enabling Vim's 'secure' option (:help "secure"), which disables dangerous Vim script features while a local vimrc file is being sourced. However, enabling the 'secure' option also limits what you can achieve in your local vimrc, making the feature less capable. On balance, I feel that local vimrc files create more problems than they solve.

Built-in Projections

Some keys have special meaning built in to the Projectionist plugin. The following table picks out some of the highlights:

Key	Purpose
path	Adds a list of directories to Vim's 'path' setting. This affects the behavior of the gf and :find commands.
make	Sets the 'makeprg' option. Additionally, it will attempt to set the 'errorformat' if a suitable compiler plugin can be found.
dispatch	Sets the b:dispatch variable. This specifies how the :Dispatch command works.
start	Sets the b:start variable. This specifies how the :Start command works.
type	Used for defining a navigation command.
alternate	Sets up an alternate file, which is used by the :A command.

The 'make', 'dispatch', and 'start' keys all support the Dispatch plugin, which I covered in Tip 10, *Running a Build and Navigating Failures*, on page 39 and Tip 11, *Switching Compilers*, on page 46.

The 'type' key is used heavily in Tip 8, *Finding Files Semantically*, on page 30, while the 'alternate' key is used in Tip 9, *Jumping to an Alternate File*, on page 35.

It's hard to give an elevator pitch on what makes the Projectionist plugin so useful. Hopefully you can see now that it provides the glue that binds together lots of important bits of functionality.

What's Next for Modern Vim?

Most technical books go out of date soon after they are published, or even before they hit the shelves! My first book, *Practical Vim*, is a rare exception. In that book, I chose to focus on Vim's core features. And because Vim has been around since the early 1990s, it's a mature and stable piece of software.

But Vim continues to evolve. With the release of version 8, Vim gained exciting new abilities. I wanted to write about some of those new features, but I felt that they were out of scope for *Practical Vim*. That's how the idea for writing *Modern Vim* came about.

In this book I'm writing about a moving target. (Just like most technical books!) While *Practical Vim* remains evergreen, this edition of *Modern Vim* is likely to go out of date before long, and I already have ideas about what I want to write about in the next edition of this book. In this appendix, I want to share with you what excites me about the future of Vim and Neovim.

Integrating with the Language Server Protocol

The implementation of certain language-specific features requires deep knowledge of the target language. I'm talking about features like jump to definition, auto-completion, and showing in-place contextual information such as function signatures or documentation. For want of a better term, I'm going to group these together and refer to them as "Rich Language" features.

To implement a useful "jump to definition" feature, you need to be able to identify the core constructs of that language, whether they're called functions, methods, classes, modules, or whatever. You also need to be able to locate the file and line number where a construct is defined, which requires knowledge of how the target language loads code from external files. Each language has its own conventions, so the implementation of this feature would be different for each language.

Suppose you want to add these Rich Language features when working with TypeScript in Vim. You could use Vim script to encode all of that TypeScript-specific knowledge. That would give you the features you want in Vim, but only in Vim. If you wanted to attract open-source contributions (bug-fixes, new features, and so on), you'd have to appeal to programmers who know both TypeScript and Vim script. That's a relatively small pool of potential contributors. Parcelling up TypeScript functionality into silos that only work with a single text editor is a bit of a dead end.

Alternatively, you could create an editor-agnostic *Language Server* that implements the TypeScript-specific features. This would run in a process of its own, providing an application programming interface (API) that would allow any text editor to interface with it. You could implement the Language Server using any language of your choice, but TypeScript would be the obvious choice. Anyone with TypeScript knowledge could potentially submit patches for bug fixes and new features. Those improvements would then be available to all users, regardless of their choice of text editor.

This approach is fairly common today. To name a couple of examples: Alchemist-server provides Rich Language features for Elixir,[1] and Tern provides Rich Language features for JavaScript.[2] You can install a Vim plugin to hook up with Tern, and you can install another Vim plugin to work with Alchemist. Likewise, you could find similar plugins to make these engines work with other text editors. It's great that these tools can be used with different text editors, but there's still a sore point: Alchemist and Tern each have completely different APIs.

Wouldn't it be cool if there was a standardized protocol for these kinds of editor-agnostic tools? The folks at Microsoft have designed the Language Server Protocol (LSP) to meet this need.[3] Here's the promise: If your text editor speaks LSP, then you can add Rich Language features for any programming language simply by installing the appropriate Language Server.

Microsoft first announced LSP in June 2016.[4] Since then, Language Servers have emerged for dozens of different programming languages, and a handful

---

1.   https://github.com/tonini/alchemist-server
2.   https://github.com/ternjs/tern
3.   https://github.com/Microsoft/language-server-protocol/blob/gh-pages/specification.md
4.   https://code.visualstudio.com/blogs/2016/06/27/common-language-protocol

of text editors have gained LSP clients. You can find a comprehensive list online.[5]

I'm rooting for LSP! If the technology gains widespread adoption then it could unlock Rich Language features for lots of different text editors. The job control APIs in Vim 8 and Neovim make it possible for these editors to communicate asynchronously with Language Servers, which is crucial for providing a good user experience.

This topic naturally falls within the scope of *Modern Vim*. In truth, LSP was largely responsible for motivating me to write this book. So why haven't I written about it in this edition? I just need more time. The technology is still new, and it's not yet clear to me what's the best way to use LSP in Vim 8 and Neovim.

If you can't wait for the next edition and you want to try out LSP in Vim for yourself, there are several resources to explore. LanguageClient-neovim,[6] by Junfeng Li, is currently the most well-established LSP plugin. This is implemented in Python as a remote plugin. The author's original intention was to support Neovim only, but people have found clever ways of making this work in Vim 8, too. You'll find advice on how to install this plugin on GitHub.[7]

vim-lsp,[8] by Prabir Shrestha, is another promising LSP plugin. This one is designed to work in Vim 8 and Neovim. There's also vim-lsc[9] by Nate Bosch. Finally, TJ DeVries is working on adding built-in LSP support to Neovim. You can view the work-in-progress pull request on GitHub.[10]

As you can see, there's lots of excitement around LSP in the Vim and (especially) Neovim communities. Having so many options is overwhelming at the moment, but with competition, some of these projects may thrive.

What's Next for Vim 8

Vim's pace of development has really picked up since the Neovim fork was created. Neovim was first to introduce features such as job control and a terminal emulator, but Vim 8 is catching up. It seems as though the competition has benefited both projects.

---

5. https://langserver.org
6. https://github.com/autozimu/LanguageClient-neovim
7. https://github.com/autozimu/LanguageClient-neovim/blob/master/INSTALL.md
8. https://github.com/prabirshrestha/vim-lsp
9. https://github.com/natebosch/vim-lsc
10. https://github.com/neovim/neovim/pull/6856

Adding :terminal support

In July 2017, Bram Moolenaar added patch 8.0.0693 to Vim introducing a basic implementation of a :terminal command. I'll admit that it took me by surprise. Not least because Vim's documentation (:help design-not) has long stated that:

> Vim is not a shell or an Operating System. *You will not be able to run a shell inside Vim* or use it to control a debugger. This should work the other way around: Use Vim as a component from a shell or in an IDE.

The philosophy of Vim's design could be summarized: Vim may be hosted inside another program, but it may not act as host to other programs. This constraint has guided the way that we use Vim for years. Introducing a :terminal command goes against this foundational design decision, and makes it possible to do things that were previously impossible. I'm watching with interest to see how this feature evolves.

At the time of writing, the :terminal command is still a work in progress. It's not yet stable enough for me to write about, but I hope to be able to cover the feature in a later edition of this book if the feature turns out to be useful. I can speculate about how some of the topics discussed in this book will be affected by this new feature.

If you want to use the fzf plugin in GVim, you currently have to configure the plugin to launch an external terminal emulator. (This is not required when you run Terminal Vim, because fzf can use the host terminal.) When the :terminal command becomes available, it will be possible for GVim to use the built-in terminal emulator instead of an external emulator. Junegunn Choi, author of fzf, has already added experimental support for this feature, so you can try it out now if you're curious!

It's unlikely the terminal feature in Vim 8 will be compatible with the equivalent feature in Neovim. That's bad news for users, for plugin authors, and for anyone writing a book about modern Vim.

What's Next for Neovim

Neovim is an ambitious project. In the following sections, I'll discuss some of the features that you can expect to see in a future release of Neovim.

Externalizing the User Interface

Vim's user interface (UI) can appear differently depending on the environment in which it runs. Most commonly, Vim runs inside a terminal user interface

(TUI), where everything must be rendered using ASCII text. You can also run Vim within a graphical user interface (GUI), where certain parts of the interface can be rendered using graphical elements.

To begin with, we'll look closely at Vim's tab bar. This UI element has had the capability to be rendered graphically since version 7.0 of Vim, making this example relevant for both Vim 8 and Neovim. Next, we'll consider other parts of the UI that could benefit from similar treatment. Externalizing these UI elements is on Neovim's roadmap.

The Tab Bar

By default, the tab bar becomes visible at the top of the screen when you open two or more tab pages. It lets you know how many tab pages are open and which one is currently active. If you have mouse support enabled, you can select or rearrange the tab pages by clicking or dragging the items in the tab bar.

When Vim runs inside a TUI, it renders the tab bar using ASCII text. Inside a GUI, the tab bar is rendered as a graphical widget. Compare how these look in the following figure (terminal Vim is on the top; MacVim is on the bottom):

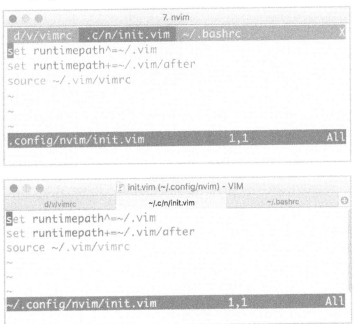

These differ in appearance, but the functionality is the same. In the TUI, the ASCII tab bar is your only option. But in the GUI, you can have it whichever way you like (:set guioptions-=e will disable the graphical tab bar).

GVim has had the capability for a long time to render a graphical tab bar, instead of showing the ASCII text version. Other parts of Vim's user interface could benefit from being rendered graphically. In the next section, we'll consider the pop-up menu.

The Pop-Up Menu

Vim's pop-up menu (PUM) appears when you invoke completion, for example, by pressing `<C-n>` in Insert mode. The PUM presents you with a list of options, allowing you to select an item and insert it into the document at the current cursor position. You can see how it looks in the following figure:

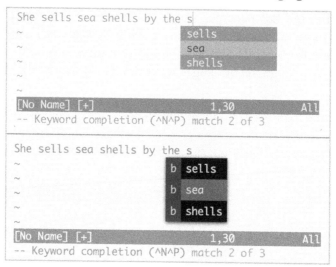

The top screenshot shows how the PUM looks in terminal Vim: it's constrained to a grid whose cell dimensions are determined by the font size. The colors of the selected item and the other items are determined by the active color scheme. With Vim 8, the pop-up menu always looks the same, whether running in the terminal or in a GUI. But Neovim has made it so that the PUM can be rendered externally by a GUI.

The bottom screenshot shows the same scene using a Neovim GUI called gonvim,[11] which renders the PUM using a graphical widget. This version of the PUM is not constrained to the ASCII grid, so the font size and line spacing can be changed independently from those used elsewhere in the UI.

This opens up new possibilities. For example, suppose you configured Neovim so that when you invoke completion, each suggestion in the menu has some associated metadata. Instead of simply showing a list of possible completions,

---

11. https://github.com/dzhou121/gonvim

the PUM could display the metadata alongside each suggestion. In this screenshot, each item in the menu is prefixed with the letter "b," which indicates that the suggestion was generated by scanning the list of open buffers.

Tiled Windows and Status Line

With Vim you can divide your workspace into a tiled layout by creating vertical or horizontal splits. Vim draws dividing lines between windows using ASCII characters: a line of | characters separates vertical splits, while horizontal splits are divided with a status line. That's appropriate in the context of a TUI environment, but what about in a GUI? Wouldn't it be neat if the graphical environment could take care of rendering the tiling windows? For example, the GUI could use a visual effect to highlight the window that is currently active (or to de-emphasize the inactive windows). Neovim plans to externalize the window drawing UI, which would make it possible for GUIs to do this.

Vim's status line appears at the bottom of each split window. By default, the status line shows the file path of the current buffer. You can customize this to show other information, such as the name of the current branch if you're working in a Git repository.

The Vim-Airline plugin[12] customizes the appearance of Vim's status line in a way that's quite eye-catching. To achieve this effect, not only do you have to install the Vim plugin, but you also need to install a patched font and use it in your terminal. On GitHub, you can find a repository of patched fonts for various monospaced fonts.[13] Using a patched font in your terminal gives you the capability to use icons that wouldn't otherwise be available in a TUI environment. That's a pretty ingenious hack!

Alternatively, imagine if you could simply ask the GUI to render the status line. Neovim plans to externalize the status line rendering, so that in a GUI environment, you could render whatever graphical icons you please. Given the popularity of the Vim-Airline plugin (with more than 10,000 stars on GitHub), it seems likely that this would be a good selling point for running Neovim in a GUI.

GUIs for Neovim

One of the goals of the Neovim project is to make it possible to create better GUIs by externalizing some of the UI. The Neovim core team doesn't maintain a GUI, but you can find a list of GUIs on the Related Projects wiki page.[14]

---

12. https://github.com/vim-airline/vim-airline
13. https://github.com/powerline/fonts
14. https://github.com/neovim/neovim/wiki/Related-projects#gui

At present, most of the GUIs for Neovim are experimental projects. These come in various different flavors. For example, Gonvim is implemented using GoLang with the QT graphical framework.[15] Oni is an Electron app, implemented using TypeScript.[16] VimR uses the Cocoa framework for macOS and is implemented in Swift and Objective C.[17] Each of these GUIs has some neat features that really differentiate it from the terminal Vim experience. If you're curious, I recommend trying them out.

There's a radical alternative way to create a Neovim GUI: embedding it inside of another text editor. Let's explore this idea in the next section.

Embedding Neovim in Other Editors

You can find Vim-emulation plugins for many text editors. These usually work by implementing a subset of Vim's features. When you begin using a Vim-emulation plugin, it's usually a matter of minutes before you discover a command that's missing, or whose behavior differs subtly from the equivalent command in Vim. As a result, these Vim-emulation plugins often fall into the "uncanny valley," making them somewhat unsatisfying to use.

Instead of reimplementing Vim's features from scratch, what if you could actually embed Vim inside of another text editor? Imagine if your Vim emulator actually loaded the settings from your vimrc and used any Vim plugins you had installed? Neovim makes this possible.

Sublime Text[18] and Virtual Studio Code[19] are both programmer's text editors that are available for Linux, Windows, and macOS. Each of these editors can embed Neovim, if you install the right plugin.

ActualVim for Sublime Text 3

Sublime Text 3 ships with a Vim-emulation plugin called *Vintage mode*, which is disabled by default. If you want to use Vim-style commands in Sublime Text, you simply have to enable the Vintage mode plugin.

Alternatively, you could install ActualVim,[20] by Ryan Hileman. This plugin actually embeds an instance of Neovim inside Sublime Text (hence the name

---

15. https://github.com/dzhou121/gonvim
16. https://github.com/onivim/oni
17. https://github.com/qvacua/vimr
18. https://www.sublimetext.com
19. https://code.visualstudio.com
20. https://github.com/lunixbochs/actualvim

ActualVim!). You get to use all the features of Sublime Text in combination with true Vim commands.

VSCodeVim for VSCode

You can enable Vim emulation for VSCode by installing the VSCodeVim plugin.[21] Like most Vim emulators, this plugin simulates a subset of Vim's Normal mode commands. Optionally, you can configure the plugin to embed an instance of Neovim. By doing so, you get to use Ex commands such as :substitute, :global, and :normal. The plugin doesn't emulate these commands; it delegates them to the embedded Neovim instance.

In its current form, the VSCodeVim plugin uses a mixture of the two approaches: emulation for Normal mode commands and delegation for Ex commands. One of the main contributors to the plugin, Horace He, is now rewriting it so as to use an embedded Neovim instance for Normal mode commands as well. Stripping out the Vim emulation code makes for a much smaller codebase. It's still a work in progress, but if you want to try it out you can find the VSCodeNeovim repository on GitHub.[22]

Challenges of Embedding Neovim

When you embed Neovim inside of a host text editor, there are bound to be some features that overlap. For example, tab pages and split windows are commonly used for organizing your workspace within a text editor. Neovim supports these features, and if you embed Neovim inside a host editor that supports similar features, then you'll have two overlapping feature sets for organizing your workspace. That could be pretty confusing for users. To keep things simple, it would make sense to disable commands such as :split, :vsplit, and :tabedit in the embedded instance of Neovim, leaving the host text editor in charge of managing your workspace.

Another basic feature that will likely overlap between the host editor and the embedded Neovim instance is undo. Allowing both text editors to keep track of the undo history could lead to strange results, especially if the editors have different ideas about what counts as an "undoable" change. Once again, putting either the host editor or the embedded Neovim instance in charge of this feature would make for better usability.

When implementing a traditional Vim-emulator plugin, you typically have to make a decision over which parts of Vim's functionality to re-implement from

---

21. https://github.com/VSCodeVim/Vim
22. https://github.com/chillee/vscodeneovim

scratch. Whereas when implementing a plugin that embeds Neovim, instead you have to decide which parts of Vim's functionality you want to surface and which parts you need to hide. That's a different kind of challenge.

Making Neovim embeddable is one of the major goals of the Neovim project. As I write this, Sublime Text and VSCode are the only text editors that can embed Neovim, but I expect to see similar plugins for other text editors soon. Anyone who wants to try embedding Neovim inside another text editor can use the ActualVim and VSCodeVim plugins as reference material.

Throughout this book, I've presented various tips to show how you can turn Vim into a development environment. The fact that Neovim can be embedded inside other text editors presents an alternative approach. You can use the host text editor as your development environment, while using Vim's modal input model for the mechanical act of editing text. To put it another way: instead of *turning* Vim into an IDE, you can *bring* Vim into your IDE.

Bibliography

[Hog16]   Brian P. Hogan. *tmux 2*. The Pragmatic Bookshelf, Raleigh, NC, 2016.

[Nei15]   Drew Neil. *Practical Vim, Second Edition*. The Pragmatic Bookshelf, Raleigh, NC, 2015.

Index

Thank you!

How did you enjoy this book? Please let us know. Take a moment and email us at support@pragprog.com with your feedback. Tell us your story and you could win free ebooks. Please use the subject line "Book Feedback."

Ready for your next great Pragmatic Bookshelf book? Come on over to https://pragprog.com and use the coupon code BUYANOTHER2018 to save 30% on your next ebook.

Void where prohibited, restricted, or otherwise unwelcome. Do not use ebooks near water. If rash persists, see a doctor. Doesn't apply to *The Pragmatic Programmer* ebook because it's older than the Pragmatic Bookshelf itself. Side effects may include increased knowledge and skill, increased marketability, and deep satisfaction. Increase dosage regularly.

And thank you for your continued support,

Andy Hunt, Publisher.

Pragmatic Bookshelf

SAVE 30%!
Use coupon code
BUYANOTHER2018

Long Live the Command Line!

Use tmux and Vim for incredible mouse-free productivity.

tmux 2

Your mouse is slowing you down. The time you spend context switching between your editor and your consoles eats away at your productivity. Take control of your environment with tmux, a terminal multiplexer that you can tailor to your workflow. With this updated second edition for tmux 2.3, you'll customize, script, and leverage tmux's unique abilities to craft a productive terminal environment that lets you keep your fingers on your keyboard's home row.

Brian P. Hogan
(102 pages) ISBN: 9781680502213. $21.95
https://pragprog.com/book/bhtmux2

The VimL Primer

Build on your editor's capabilities and tailor your editing experience with VimL, the powerful scripting language built into Vim. With VimL you can configure basic settings or add entirely new functionality. Use this quick and easy introduction to create your own Vim plugin while learning the concepts and syntax of VimL.

Benjamin Klein
(82 pages) ISBN: 9781680500400. $17
https://pragprog.com/book/bkviml

Fix Your Hidden Problems

From technical debt to deployment in the very real, very messy world, we've got the tools you need to fix the hidden problems before they become disasters.

Software Design X-Rays

Are you working on a codebase where cost overruns, death marches, and heroic fights with legacy code monsters are the norm? Battle these adversaries with novel ways to identify and prioritize technical debt, based on behavioral data from how developers work with code. And that's just for starters. Because good code involves social design, as well as technical design, you can find surprising dependencies between people and code to resolve coordination bottlenecks among teams. Best of all, the techniques build on behavioral data that you already have: your version-control system. Join the fight for better code!

Adam Tornhill
(274 pages) ISBN: 9781680502725. $45.95
https://pragprog.com/book/atevol

Release It! Second Edition

A single dramatic software failure can cost a company millions of dollars—but can be avoided with simple changes to design and architecture. This new edition of the best-selling industry standard shows you how to create systems that run longer, with fewer failures, and recover better when bad things happen. New coverage includes DevOps, microservices, and cloud-native architecture. Stability antipatterns have grown to include systemic problems in large-scale systems. This is a must-have pragmatic guide to engineering for production systems.

Michael Nygard
(376 pages) ISBN: 9781680502398. $47.95
https://pragprog.com/book/mnee2

Learn Why, Then Learn How

Get started on your Elixir journey today.

Adopting Elixir

Adoption is more than programming. Elixir is an exciting new language, but to successfully get your application from start to finish, you're going to need to know more than just the language. You need the case studies and strategies in this book. Learn the best practices for the whole life of your application, from design and team-building, to managing stakeholders, to deployment and monitoring. Go beyond the syntax and the tools to learn the techniques you need to develop your Elixir application from concept to production.

Ben Marx, José Valim, Bruce Tate
(242 pages) ISBN: 9781680502527. $42.95
https://pragprog.com/book/tvmelixir

Programming Elixir ≥ 1.6

This book is *the* introduction to Elixir for experienced programmers, completely updated for Elixir 1.6 and beyond. Explore functional programming without the academic overtones (tell me about monads just one more time). Create concurrent applications, but get them right without all the locking and consistency headaches. Meet Elixir, a modern, functional, concurrent language built on the rock-solid Erlang VM. Elixir's pragmatic syntax and built-in support for metaprogramming will make you productive and keep you interested for the long haul. Maybe the time is right for the Next Big Thing. Maybe it's Elixir.

Dave Thomas
(398 pages) ISBN: 9781680502992. $47.95
https://pragprog.com/book/elixir16

More on Java

Get up to date on the latest Java 8 features, and take an in-depth look at concurrency options.

Functional Programming in Java

Get ready to program in a whole new way. *Functional Programming in Java* will help you quickly get on top of the new, essential Java 8 language features and the functional style that will change and improve your code. This short, targeted book will help you make the paradigm shift from the old imperative way to a less error-prone, more elegant, and concise coding style that's also a breeze to parallelize. You'll explore the syntax and semantics of lambda expressions, method and constructor references, and functional interfaces. You'll design and write applications better using the new standards in Java 8 and the JDK.

Venkat Subramaniam
(196 pages) ISBN: 9781937785468. $33
https://pragprog.com/book/vsjava8

Programming Concurrency on the JVM

Stop dreading concurrency hassles and start reaping the pure power of modern multicore hardware. Learn how to avoid shared mutable state and how to write safe, elegant, explicit synchronization-free programs in Java or other JVM languages including Clojure, JRuby, Groovy, or Scala.

Venkat Subramaniam
(280 pages) ISBN: 9781934356760. $35
https://pragprog.com/book/vspcon

More on Python

For data science and basic science, for you and anyone else on your team.

Data Science Essentials in Python

Go from messy, unstructured artifacts stored in SQL and NoSQL databases to a neat, well-organized dataset with this quick reference for the busy data scientist. Understand text mining, machine learning, and network analysis; process numeric data with the NumPy and Pandas modules; describe and analyze data using statistical and network-theoretical methods; and see actual examples of data analysis at work. This one-stop solution covers the essential data science you need in Python.

Dmitry Zinoviev
(224 pages) ISBN: 9781680501841. $29
https://pragprog.com/book/dzpyds

Practical Programming, Third Edition

Classroom-tested by tens of thousands of students, this new edition of the best-selling intro to programming book is for anyone who wants to understand computer science. Learn about design, algorithms, testing, and debugging. Discover the fundamentals of programming with Python 3.6—a language that's used in millions of devices. Write programs to solve real-world problems, and come away with everything you need to produce quality code. This edition has been updated to use the new language features in Python 3.6.

Paul Gries, Jennifer Campbell, Jason Montojo
(410 pages) ISBN: 9781680502688. $49.95
https://pragprog.com/book/gwpy3

The Pragmatic Bookshelf

The Pragmatic Bookshelf features books written by developers for developers. The titles continue the well-known Pragmatic Programmer style and continue to garner awards and rave reviews. As development gets more and more difficult, the Pragmatic Programmers will be there with more titles and products to help you stay on top of your game.

Visit Us Online

This Book's Home Page
https://pragprog.com/book/modvim
Source code from this book, errata, and other resources. Come give us feedback, too!

Keep Up to Date
https://pragprog.com
Join our announcement mailing list (low volume) or follow us on twitter @pragprog for new titles, sales, coupons, hot tips, and more.

New and Noteworthy
https://pragprog.com/news
Check out the latest pragmatic developments, new titles and other offerings.

Save on the eBook

Save on the eBook versions of this title. Owning the paper version of this book entitles you to purchase the electronic versions at a terrific discount.

PDFs are great for carrying around on your laptop—they are hyperlinked, have color, and are fully searchable. Most titles are also available for the iPhone and iPod touch, Amazon Kindle, and other popular e-book readers.

Buy now at *https://pragprog.com/coupon*

Contact Us

Online Orders:	*https://pragprog.com/catalog*
Customer Service:	*support@pragprog.com*
International Rights:	*translations@pragprog.com*
Academic Use:	*academic@pragprog.com*
Write for Us:	*http://write-for-us.pragprog.com*
Or Call:	+1 800-699-7764